The Complete Guide to
HIKING AND BACKPACKING

The Complete Guide to HIKING AND BACKPACKING

Edited by Andrew J. Carra

Library of Congress Cataloging in Publication Data

Main entry under title:
The Complete guide to hiking and backpacking.
    1. Backpacking 2. Hiking I. Carra, Andrew J.
GV199.6.C65   796.5   77-1514
ISBN 0-87691-226-9

Published by Winchester Press
205 East 42nd Street
New York, N.Y. 10017

Printed in the United States of America

WINCHESTER is a Trademark of Olin Corporation
used by Winchester Press, Inc. under authority and
control of the Trademark Proprietor.

Contents

Introduction

I once asked a friend why he went backpacking nearly every weekend. I wanted to know what made him drive himself to cover a certain amount of distance with a certain amount of weight on his back. Just what appealed to him?

No great, profound answer came back to me. He couldn't pinpoint what he thought he was accomplishing, nor could he tell me just what it was that excited him. All he could tell me was that he loved it. He knew he wasn't a masochist and he knew he wasn't trying to get in shape for the Olympic marathon. He just knew that he loved being out there in the wilderness, even if that wilderness was only 55 minutes from the concrete security of New York City. He enjoyed driving his body uphill and down, feeling his muscles exerting themselves, feeling the "country" air fill his lungs, feeling the feet, yards, and miles trail off behind him, knowing that everything he needed was strapped on his back. He didn't know what he was accomplishing, but he knew he was filled with a sense of self-accomplishment.

Our conversation confirmed my own suspicions that backpacking is a highly personal activity. There are no boundaries as far as accomplishment, no limits as far as time, and no scorebooks or records to be measured against. It's similar to the childhood games we all participated in. It doesn't matter which sport was your favorite, but let's say it was basketball. You were alone in your driveway or backyard—no crowds watching, no opponent guarding you, and no clock ticking down the seconds—only you and your imagination. Even without the trimmings, you would still feel a certain exhilaration at the moment the ball went tripping and snapping through the net. You were filled with a sense of appreciation.

Perhaps the appeal of backpacking lies in the sense of self that we all have. The deeper you get into the wilderness, the deeper the possibilities of getting into yourself. To me the moments in life that I am finding more and more valuable are those when I can spend some time with myself. These moments may be spent in some hidden corner of the house, during a long train or plane ride, during those dark, quiet hours just before dawn—or spent out under the stars, in the woods, alone.

The more you get into backpacking, the more you'll experience these moments. In backpacking this sense of self—this awareness of your own well being—stems from a whole world of selfs: self-reliance, self-support, self-motivation. It doesn't matter whether or not you are with someone on the trail; you'll still be able to jealously guard and appreciate those moments when you're free to get in touch with nature and yourself.

Backpacking offers a person a great deal of independence. You can go where you want, do what you want, and take as long as you want. The activity offers an escape. Lord knows, we all need to escape today. Modern technology has been intruding into more areas than we'd like. It's proving to be both a help and a hindrance in that the more we gain the more we lose. We've gained the convenience and comfort of moving from place to place in the automobile and we've lost not only the clean air our lungs crave, but too many lives as well. We have gained the "free" entertainment of television and we've lost the willingness to sit down with a book and absorb someone's lifetime of ideas.

And now we're even in danger of losing our escape routes. More and more people are finding the need to escape, finding that they have a need to get back in touch with the natural things of the earth. The wilderness, that last bastion of escape for so many of us, is now becoming overcrowded. The Appalachian Trail is starting to look like Central Park on a summer Sunday afternoon. As a result we have had to turn to legislation and quota systems to keep our lands preserved. And that has caused more problems.

There is a constant struggle going on these days about preserving

our wilderness areas. Some people are arguing that these pristine locations should not be intruded upon or disturbed so that our children
and our grandchildren may still be able to appreciate the beauty that
once was. A very noble idea. But then, what are these areas for if not
to appreciate and use them? This is what the other side is saying—let's
use them now.

There has to be some solution, some middle ground somewhere. I
don't like to see wilderness trails overrun by users. But then, neither
do I like to see these areas posted with "No Trespassing" signs. Wilderness areas are there to be appreciated; they offer an escape or alternative to today's technological world. While backpacking may not be the
answer to man's technological ills, it is an activity that gives us an out
to help us cope.

I know a person who uses the wilderness to help straighten out her
city life. To her—and within her—there is a constant appreciation of
both city and wild. At the same time there is a constant dislike of both,
too. She uses the wild to help her appreciate the convenience and com-
fortability of the city. Then, in turn, she uses the city to help her appreciate the escape—the sensual awareness—that the woods offer her.
Though the modern economic system doesn't permit her an even split,
the time she does spend away from one or the other is the time she
considers most productive in helping her cope with the life-styles. She
wouldn't have it any other way.

Both the city life and the wilderness escape give her a sense of self-
accomplishment. Both environments call for her best survival instincts.
Being out in the woods backpacking brings out this same sense of survival and accomplishment in most people. Being out there on your
own is a throwback to pioneer and, perhaps, even prehistoric times.
The psyche reaches back across eons to gather up a full appreciation
of "I did it: I have survived."

Nowadays we have all sorts of modern backpacking equipment to
help us survive—super lightweight tents and sleeping bags, prepackaged foods, sophisticated gadgetry—but there still remains within us
that psychological link. No matter how sophisticated the equipment
may be, if you carry it on your back you still retain and relate to that
instinct for self-survival. That, too, is one of the appeals. You might
have a $250 sleeping bag, a $100 pair of boots, and the most gadget-
filled collection of paraphernalia, but you're still "roughing it," still
surviving, still competing against the elements.

There's only one way to experience it, though, and that is to push yourself out the door. That's what this book is designed to help you do. It's a collection of writings by some of the most accomplished backpackers in America today. These are not people who have made reputations as survivalists. They are not expedition leaders, though they could be. These are people who enjoy backpacking and have learned how to get the most out of it. They're more fanatics than experts, doers rather than studious researchers, practical backpackers rather than laboratory technicians. Their ideas, cautions, and hints are based on years of wilderness travel. What they've done, you can do, too. All you've got to do is try.

No matter where you live there are mountains, forests, lakes, streams, or seashores to be explored by foot. There are even a number of good city trails you might want to look into if you're locked in an urban area. According to the National Park System offices there are nearly 200 wilderness areas located within 100 miles of metropolitan centers. Obviously, the opportunities are there. In the back of the book are some addresses where you can write for more information on places and products.

Wherever you decide to backpack, you might want to take the family along, too. Backpacking trips can be excellent family vacations. The whole family will be able to get away from the crowds of tourists, will be self-sustaining, and will be able to pick up and go whenever it's decided. No worries about bills to be paid, trip quotas to be met, connections to race for. A whole new world can be opened up. And look at it this way: even if the whole family except you hates the experience, it's still an experience. The next time the family goes on a tourist-type vacation, they'll appreciate *that* that much more.

If you decide to opt for the mountains—with family or without—there are some precautions that should be taken. No one expects you to go out and conquer Everest, but you should have an appreciation for changes in altitude that mountain hiking brings. Weather conditions in such regions are extremely volatile. The higher altitudes mean lower temperatures and an increased exposure to ultraviolet rays of the sun. Precautions should be taken for both sun stroke and hypothermia (see Chapter 13). Just be sure you become acquainted with high-altitude guidelines. Taking a few moments to go over basic warning signals or taking along a bit of extra protective gear can save you a great amount of hardship later on.

Mountain hiking is usually slower going than traveling along lower elevation trails. That's only natural. You'll be running up against cliffs, outcroppings of rocks, steep grades, and uneven footing. Expect it to take a lot out of you if you're not used to it. You'll use up much more energy in mountain country because of the constant climbing. And when this exertion is combined with harsher weather conditions and, perhaps, a significant change in altitude, mountain travel can certainly lose much of its appeal, no matter how many scenic vistas you come across.

Generally speaking, though, there is little difference between walking along a relatively level wilderness trail and walking in the mountains. It isn't until you get into mountains such as the Rockies that you need further guidance and instruction. Unless you're planning on a midwinter, three-day expedition in any of the northern mountainous areas, an average amount of caution should do for walking the hills. If you stay below the timberline and use common sense, you'll stand a much better chance of experiencing an enjoyable backpacking trip rather than undergoing a wilderness survival adventure.

Similar precautions apply to desert hiking. The tips found in Chapter 12 on seasonal hiking hold up well for desert hiking and there is really no need to go into all the distinctions and variations of desert and mountain backpacking. Be content to stay within reasonable terrain for your first few trips. The more you find yourself enjoying the activity, the more you can be searching out more treacherous terrains and environments.

What holds for where you backpack also holds for when you should backpack. Be as sure as you reasonably can be about weather conditions before you venture out. Take into consideration altitude, season of the year, terrain, short- and long-range weather forecasts, and, of course, bring along necessary gear for all contingencies. You'll find that the Boy Scouts were right all along—Be Prepared.

When gearing yourself up for backpacking don't rush out and buy the highest-quality and highest-priced equipment just because you think you might enjoy the activity. Being overequipped can be just as bad as being underequipped. If you can, put yourself in the hands of some good, local wilderness outfitters. These people—usually—are not out to oversell you. More often than not, they'll talk you down from what you think you will need. Tell them the type of backpacking or hiking you're planning and let them outfit you to your scale of ability and to your pocketbook. Even if you plan to buy your equipment through a mail-order house or in a department store, you would do well to visit a specialty shop and ask a few questions. Most shops can set you up with rented equipment, just so you can get a feel for the activity without the initial capital investment. If you're a novice, your best bet is to rent. Then, once you're sure of what you like and don't like, you'll be in a much better position to make a decision about buying.

If you are a backpacker, or are planning to take up the sport, follow the advice given in this book. The chapters on equipment are important to you and your buying habits. So, too, are those sections devoted to skills and personal well being. Just as important as all this, however, is the underlying message that each writer is conveying between the lines. Each has a full appreciation of the wilderness, and with that appreciation comes respect for the environment. Beneath all the advice on equipment and all the practical hints on the activity is a love of the wilderness.

There is an old adage that is stated in nearly every book on backpacking and wilderness travel: "Leave nothing but footprints; take nothing but pictures (or memories)." But these writers agree that the adage should be expanded these days. Take out of the wilderness *more* than you brought in—both physically and mentally. Pack out someone else's leavings and repair someone else's mistakes. Be generous and be vigorous. If we all start cleaning up our wilderness areas and our attitudes toward our fellow beings, we'll be a lot better off in the future.

PART I

What You Need

1

Boots

by Dave Engerbretson

In contrast to only a few years ago, today's backpackers are confronted by a vast array of specialized equipment and clothing from which to select their personal gear. For the average hiker, much of this equipment is unnecessary, and unwary buyers can quickly find themselves inundated by pounds and pounds of "lightweight" accessories. On the other hand, certain items such as packs, sleeping bags, and footwear are basic to everyone's needs.

Of these basic pieces of equipment, the footwear is without a doubt the most important item to be purchased by the serious backpacker. The hiker's feet must perform almost herculean tasks on even the most routine outing. While carrying weights far in excess of their normal load, the feet slam into the ground thousands of times every day over terrain that is rough, smooth, dry, wet, loose, solid, uneven, and ever changing. The feet must carry out these tasks without slipping and without pain day after day. The safety and very survival of every member of the group literally depends upon the feet of each individual. Thus, the selection of the appropriate footwear is vitally important for safe and enjoyable backpacking.

Even the casual window shopper will soon discover that a bewildering number of types, styles, and prices of boots and shoes is available to the backpacker. However, with a little knowledge of boot types and construction methods, the selection process need not be unnecessarily traumatic, and you can be assured of obtaining a boot of high quality that is well suited to your specific needs.

Types of Footwear

Despite the wide range of styles, most camping and backpacking footwear can be placed into one of five categories, based upon intended use: (1) camp shoes, (2) trail shoes, (3) hiking boots, (4) climbing boots and kletterschue, and (5) mountaineering boots. When choosing footwear, it is essential to understand the differences between these categories, and to select something that is designed to perform the tasks you will be giving it.

Camp shoes are not really boots at all, but are soft, lightweight shoes that are only worn while in camp. Such footwear offers protection to the feet when heavier hiking boots are not required, and are a joy to slip into at the end of a hard day on the trail. The most common shoe for this purpose is the ubiquitous canvas tennis shoe or sneaker, but others range from lightweight oxfords with thin lug soles to rubber sandals.

Since camp shoes are really extra items to be carried in the pack,

Two types of shoes that are ideal for in-camp use. At the top is the Eddie Bauer Canoe Moccasin and below is the Russell Oneida double-soled moccasin.

primary considerations are their weight and compactness. My own personal favorites are the tough little soleless moccasins often sold under the name "canoe moccasin." Sneakers, however, are better suited for stream crossings in order to keep your hiking boots dry, and they can be used in an emergency for actual hiking. Thus, whether I carry sneakers or my pet moccasins is determined by the nature and location of a given trip.

Trail shoes are not intended for serious backpacking with heavy loads over rough ground. Rather, they are soft, lightweight, high-topped shoes to be worn on gentle "trail walks" where firm support is unnecessary. Such shoes will have a variety of rubber or crepe soles.

Catalogs list trail shoes under various names (trail boots, walkers, walking boots, light boots, etc.), but all will be classified as "light-weight." Weight per pair can be expected to be in the neighborhood of 3 pounds, and prices range from under $20 to slightly over $40. Trail shoes are ideally suited to their purpose, but they should not be expected to perform the function of an "all-around" hiking boot.

Lightweight trail boots are made by a number of manufacturers, including J. C. Penney. This "Lug Boot" has a cemented welt but no midsole. It's not made for carrying great amounts of weight, but serves nicely for day hikes over easy terrain.

Hiking boots are the ideal boots for the majority of recreational backpackers. Often sold under the name "medium-weight hiking" or "lightweight climbing" boots, they offer the type of support, foot protection, and traction required by the backpacker who carries moderate to heavy loads under a wide range of conditions. True hiking boots are relatively stiff due to the heavier leathers and sole construction, and require a certain amount of breaking in. These boots feature a variety of hard rubber lug soles, and weigh about 4 to 5 pounds per pair for men and slightly less for women. Excellent boots are also available in this category for children.

High-quality, medium-weight hiking boots are currently priced in the $40 to $80 range. Children's sizes are slightly less. The escalating cost of prime bootmaking leather will undoubtedly cause prices of boots to continue to rise. Top-quality boots, however, can be expected to last many years if given reasonable care, and should be considered an investment in backpacking safety and comfort. They are worth the price even if it means scrimping a little on certain other pieces of equipment.

Though at opposite poles of the construction spectrum, *climbing boots* and *kletterschue* can be placed in the same functional category. Climbing boots, at first glance, appear to be very similar to the hiking boots discussed above. There are important differences, however, that should preclude the use of climbing boots for general hiking and backpacking.

Climbing boots are designed for rugged off-trail use, usually in technical rock and ice climbing, where the foot requires a great deal of protection and support. Therefore, these boots are made of much heavier leather, with stiffer soles, and often with different construction methods. Due to their stiffness, they require much more breaking in before they are comfortable. And they are heavy, usually in the 5- to 6-plus-pound range.

Kletterschue are also to be used only for technical rock climbing, but are designed to be very lightweight, tight fitting, and stripped of any frills that might snag or hang up when the foot is jammed into a rock crack. These shoes are built with very stiff narrow soles, and a rather unique construction. Though they are sometimes sold as lightweight trail shoes, they should never be used for this purpose. Kletterschue offer little or no protection or support for the hiker and should be used only by technical friction climbers.

Top
The Pivetta 8 is a mediumweight hiking and backpacking boot. Note the Littleway welt construction and closely cropped sole.

Above
The Vasque Hiker II is a mediumweight backpacking boot that features a combination of D-ring and speed lacing.

The Kletterschue is a technical climbing shoe. Note the lightweight construction, closely cropped soles, and high-friction smooth soles. At the left is the Galibier Super and on the right is the Galibier Yosemite.

Mountaineering boots are built for the most rugged off-trail rock and ice climbing and expeditionary work, and are totally unsuited for use by the recreational backpacker. Often utilizing a double boot construction and various types of insulation, such boots are extremely stiff and heavy, and may weigh in excess of 7 pounds per pair. Fortunately, their high cost and obviously heavy construction usually eliminate them from consideration by the hiker.

Boot Construction

Since hiking boots are made by a number of companies in all parts of the world, it is not too surprising that their construction and materials vary considerably. Though different models may look similar to the casual observer, one may be significantly inferior to the other. The customer who is unable to judge the difference stands a good chance of receiving neither the full value for his dollar nor full performance from his boots.

A major factor in boot quality is the leather used by the manufacturer. As the hide comes from the animal and is tanned, it is usually

Top
For many beginning backpackers a standard field boot will do nicely. Here's the Bauer 6-inch model, which would come under the category of lightweight trail shoes.

Above
For the experts there is the expedition-type mountaineering boot. This comes with a separate fleece lining that is removable. The expedition-type boots are a bit beyond the needs of the average backpacker.

split into layers. The outer layer, i.e., that which was next to the animal's hair, is called "top grain," while all others are called "split grain" or simply "splits." Split-grain leathers have less strength and natural water repellency than top grains. They tend to stretch, and are much less durable, making them quite inferior for hiking boots. Split-grain leather can usually be identified by a suedelike appearance.

Boots of top-grain leather may have either a smooth or rough finish (not to be confused with the softer, finer grained suede), and both types have their advocates. The "rough-out," top-grain boots are possibly a little more durable than those with a smooth finish since the smooth surface is placed on the inside of the boot where it is protected from damage. The "rough-out" surface absorbs waterproofing agents very well and produces a relatively dry boot.

Boot leather is generally tanned by either the chrome or the oil (vegetable) tanning process. The chrome method produces a dry, hard finish, while the oil method yields a softer, oily looking leather. Top-quality boots are produced by either method.

Boot uppers can be constructed from a number of pieces of leather sewn together or from a single piece. Since seams are potential breaking points and may allow water to enter the boot, many experts prefer one-piece construction. Others believe that multipiece boots allow for a better fit. My own preference is for the one-piece style, and I have never experienced problems with fit in top-quality boots of that type.

Most boots utilize heel and toe counters between the outer leather and the lining to stiffen these areas and protect the feet, and may include a heel cap sewn outside the boot to provide additional protection at this point of wear. The heel and toe counters protect the feet from bruises and other injuries, while the heel cap's function is more debatable. But the lack of such a cap should not eliminate an otherwise excellent boot from consideration.

The degree of padding found in hiking boots varies considerably from one brand to another. The amount of padding depends a great deal upon personal preference. Those who prefer padding point to the additional comfort obtained, while opponents refer to heavily padded boots as "sweat boxes." The latter group prefers to obtain the necessary padding by using heavy socks. Also, heavily padded boots that become soaked with water are more difficult to dry than those with less padding. The best answer may well lie between either extreme.

The scree guard or padded elastic cuff that is sometimes built into the boot top in an attempt to prevent sticks, stones, dirt, and snow from getting into the boot is a debatable feature. The majority of these guards are ineffective due to the movement of the lower leg. A better solution is to wear a pair of low nylon or duck gaiters that slip over the ankle and around the outside of the boot. Such gaiters are lightweight, comfortable, and effective.

There are a number of variations in lacing methods. Most boots use either eyelets, hooks, speed lacing, or a combination of these. Eyelets are very durable and provide a smooth surface that doesn't snag. However, they are slow to lace, especially with cold or gloved hands. Hooks, on the other hand, are quick to lace but occasionally become bent or broken. Either hooks or eyelets permit "differential lacing," that is, the tension can be varied across different parts of the foot.

Speed-lacing systems usually consist of loops or D-rings through which the laces pass and can be drawn tight with a single pull. This is the fastest system, and the rings lie flat against the boot to prevent snagging. But, unless special techniques are used, such systems tend to equalize the tension and do not allow for differential lacing. Many hikers find the combination that uses speed lacing on the lower portion of the boot and hooks on the upper a happy compromise.

The use of gaiters, usually made of lightweight nylon or cotton duck cloth, effectively closes the top of the boot to dirt, stones, and sticks.

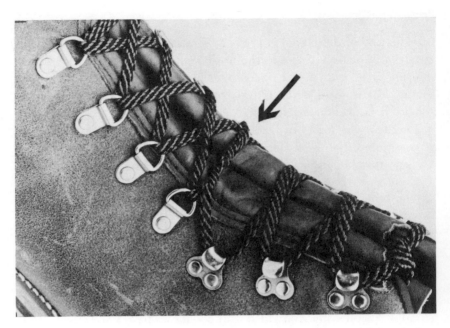

Some boots come with a combination lacing method. This model has D-ring speed lacing at the bottom and hooks at the top. Note the surgeon's knot (double overhand) at the arrow, which permits differential lacing—different amounts of tension on the lower and upper portions of the boot.

Many innovations are found in the design of boot tongues and closing systems, and almost all of the various bellows, overlapping flaps, and double tongues are quite effective. Boots with a single tongue sewn only at the bottom should be avoided, as these will often slip off to one side while hiking and leave the boot open to moisture and foreign objects. Care should be taken to see that the tongue and bellows are properly positioned and folded when lacing the boot the first few times. The tongue quickly becomes "set" in this early pattern, and if it is wrong it is very difficult to change at a later time.

Hiking boots range in height (measured from the top of the sole) from about 5 inches to 9 inches, with the average being 6 to 7. As a minimum, the boot should cover the ankle bones to provide support and protection. Maximum height is somewhat a matter of preference and intended use. A winter boot, for example, is generally higher than one that will be used only in more mild weather. A boot that is too high, however, tends to constrict the Achilles tendon and calf muscles, and may reduce the forward flexibility of the ankle. To avoid this problem, some boots are cut slightly lower in the back.

Most hiking boots come with some kind of lug sole. By far the most popular is the Vibram brand Montagnabloc.

Almost all medium-weight hiking boots will have some type of hard neoprene (rubber) lug soles. Several companies have their own particular lug pattern, but by far the most popular are those sold under the trade name of Vibram. Available in several different weights and lug patterns, Vibram soles have become the standard of the industry.

Of major importance in boot design is the welt or method used in joining the soles to the upper. A boot will have at least an inner sole and an outer sole, or, more typically, these two plus one or more leather or rubber midsoles sandwiched between them. The method used in fastening these to each other and to the upper contributes to the boot's durability, dryness, comfort, stiffness, and ease of sole replacement. Basically, one of five welts is used: cemented, injected, Littleway (inside stitched), Goodyear (U.S.), or Norwegian (storm).

A cemented welt can be identified by the lack of stitching around the top edge of the outer sole, and by the lack of a midsole. This is the least expensive welt construction as well as the least durable, and worn outer soles cannot be replaced. This type of welt is used only on light trail shoes, and should not be considered for serious hiking boots.

Injected soles are molded directly to the uppers and also have no stitching around the edge of the sole. A limited number of higher quality boots use this method, but inject only the inner and midsoles. Unless the latter method is used, the worn outer sole cannot be replaced. The key to quality in this type of construction, then, is the presence of the midsole.

Four types of welt construction: (left to right) cemented—note the absence of a midsole; Littleway—has one midsole between the boot and the lug sole; Goodyear—note the single row of stitches and the multiple midsoles; Norwegian—note the triple row of stitches and the multiple midsoles.

LITTLEWAY

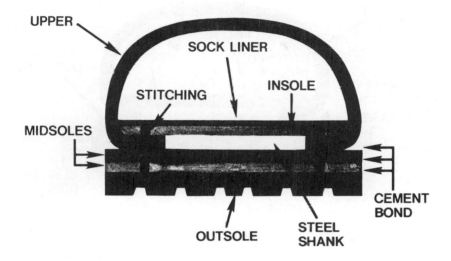

Littleway construction.

The Littleway or inside-stitched construction is very durable since the stitches are inside the boot and protected from wear and moisture. The unexposed stitching also allows the sole to be closely trimmed for use in technical climbing, and the soles are easily replaceable. Two disadvantages of this construction are that the soles tend to be especially stiff, and it does not allow the inner sole to mold to the wearer's foot as well as other welts.

The majority of hiking, climbing, and mountaineering boots utilize either the Goodyear or Norwegian welt in which the upper is stitched to the inner and midsoles. The outer lug sole is then glued (and often also screwed or nailed) to the midsole, and can easily be replaced when necessary. As can be seen in the illustration (next page), the design of the Norwegian welt eliminates one seam and is thought by some to be a little more water resistant. The Goodyear welt can be recognized by the single row of stitching running around the top edge of the sole, whereas the Norwegian welt has two, or in the case of some mountaineering boots, three rows of stitching. Either of these two perform very well, and the use of one or the other should not be the cause of rejecing an otherwise perfect boot.

GOODYEAR WELT

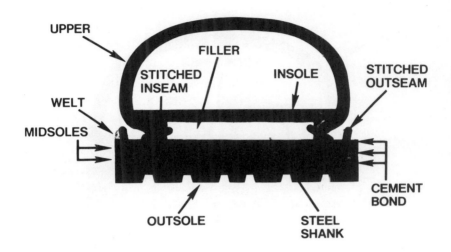

NORWEGIAN WELT

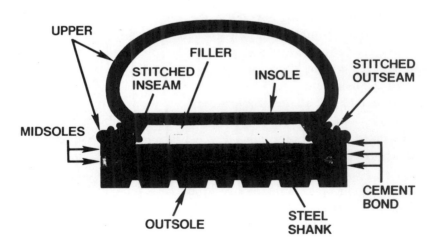

Goodyear welt construction.

Norwegian welt construction.

Selecting and Fitting the Boot

The "ideal" all-around boot for the "average" hiker or backpacker will be classed as a medium-weight hiking boot, and will weigh from just under 4 to about 5 pounds per pair. It will be roughly 6 to 7 inches in height, and will be made of either smooth or rough-out top-grain leather with a minimum number of seams. The uppers will be moderately stiff with a hard toe and heel, and the soles, while they'll feel stiff to the hand, should flex comfortably when worn. The Vibram or similar lug soles will be fastened to fairly thick inner and midsoles with either a Goodyear or Norwegian welt. Other features such as scree collars, inner padding, heel caps, tongue design, and lacing method are up to individual tastes and comfort requirements. Though more expensive boots are available, our "ideal" will probably cost between $40 and $60.

As important as the above considerations are, there is one major criterion for purchasing hiking boots—fit. A boot that meets every other requirement is useless if it doesn't fit properly, and the buyer should be prepared to sacrifice some other feature if necessary to obtain a pair that fits correctly. Don't rely on a boot "stretching out to fit" as it is used or on making adjustments of socks to obtain comfort. *The basic fit of the boot must be correct before it is purchased!*

The choice of the correct socks is almost as important as the choice of boots, and this decision should be made before being fitted for boots. (See Chapter 2 for a discussion of the correct kinds of socks to be worn when hiking and backpacking.)

Several factors must be considered when fitting boots. They must be long enough so the toes will not be jammed into the leather when walking downhill, and they must not be so tight that the toes are cramped and can easily become chilled. At the same time, the boot must be tight enough at both the toe and the heel to prevent the boot from slipping, creating friction and causing blisters. In other words, the boot must be loose but not too loose, tight but not too tight. Fortunately, solving this problem is not as difficult as it sounds.

First, the boot should be fitted for length; normally this will be at least a half size larger than your street shoes. While wearing the sock combination you have selected, place your foot into the boot and jam it forward until the toes touch the front of the boot. At this point, you should just be able to slip your index finger down between your heel and the heel of the boot. If this cannot be done, the boots are too short, and, if more than one finger can be inserted, they are too long. Try different sizes until this dimension is correct. Incidentally, always try to wear new socks while fitting boots as they will be a little more bulky than socks that have been well worn.

If the boots are the right length and seem reasonably comfortable for width across the ball of the foot, lace them tightly, and proceed to the next step. If it feels as though they will be either painfully tight or much too loose, try a different pair before lacing.

With the boots tightly laced, check to see how close the sides of the front opening are from each other. They should be far enough apart to allow for future tightening of the boot after the leather has stretched or while wearing a lighter sock combination. If the boots are of the overlapping "split-tongue" design, be certain that there is a minimum of $3/8$ths of an inch between the edge of the tongue flap and the lacing hooks on the opposite side.

The boot should now feel snug but comfortable. You should be able to wriggle your toes, but there should be no lateral movement across the ball of the foot. Boots may stretch and become a bit wider during use, but don't count on this to make a poorly fitting boot feel comfortable. If the boot checks out okay so far, stand firmly on the floor and have a friend or the salesperson grip it at the toe and heel while you attempt to lift your heel away from the inner sole. You should be unable to lift it by more than $1/8$th of an inch. Movement greater than this will lead to blisters and a sore Achilles tendon. While the boot is still being held firmly, try twisting and slipping and sliding your foot around inside to check again for a sloppy fit.

Now make a final check for length by "scuffing" your foot forward and stopping it quickly to see if your toes jam forward against the boot. Better yet, try standing on a steep incline if one can be found and try to jam your toes forward. This tendency will be greatly increased while walking downhill carrying a heavy pack, so check it out thoroughly before buying the boots.

Finally, put on both boots and stroll around the store for a while. A half hour is not too long when you're down to your final boot choice. During your walk, check them out for general comfort and "feel," and be certain that no irritating sore spots develop.

If you're reasonably sure of the fit at this point, buy them. But make certain that the shop will let you return them within a couple of days if they don't feel right to you after wearing them around the house (not outside!) . Most shops will be happy to do this if the boots show no signs of wear.

Don't hesitate to take plenty of time in the shop while trying on boots. Good boots are an investment in backpacking comfort and safety, and the purchase should not be a hasty one. Try as many different brands of boots as possible, since there will probably be a difference in fit even though they are the same size. And, for goodness sake, be willing either to give up a few features or move up to a slightly more expensive model if necessary to obtain the perfect fit.

Since fit is so important, it is best to buy the boot in person whenever possible. Even if it means delaying the purchase or making a long trip to a shop, you should avoid ordering by mail unless absolutely necessary. If you do have to order boots by mail, the following procedure should increase your chances of obtaining a good fit, though it may take a couple of tries. First, while wearing your hiking socks, stand firmly on a piece of white paper or cardboard with both feet. Using a pencil or felt-tipped pen, trace around the outside of your largest foot, taking care to keep the pen absolutely vertical. Label the drawing with your name, address, and normal shoe size; cut it out and enclose it with your order form. Any reputable company will normally allow you to return mail-ordered boots in unworn condition, but be certain to state in your order not to ship the boots if this practice is not permitted.

But suppose that you are one of those with real problem feet—a size 8AAAA or 14EEE, or one of those with some odd bumps where they don't belong. Are you out of luck? Not at all.

Excellent custom-made boots are available at quite reasonable cost from several bootmakers in the United States. Names and addresses of some of them can be obtained in the advertisements of most backpacking magazines, but the one I am most familiar with is Limmer & Sons, Intervale, New Hampshire. At $70 per pair, custom-made Limmers are quite likely the best buy on the market. Mine were resoled and had the midsole rebuilt after 12 years of hard use, and now look virtually as good as new.

But, as they say, there's good news and there's bad news. The bad news is that, with practically no advertising other than satisfied customers, the Limmer boot has become so popular around the world that the current waiting time for delivery is three years. The good news is that they have recently begun to have an identical boot made for them by a reputable German firm, and this one sells for $60 with no waiting time. The latter, which is not custom made, of course, comes with the usual perfect fit guaranteed, and, according to Peter Limmer, Jr., is indistinguishable from original models. Limmer also has a few of its handmade boots in stock that customers have failed to pick up, and if these happen to be your size you're in luck. Limmers will provide instructions for measuring your feet for either the custom-made or the German boot, and, as I said, they're guaranteed to fit. It's an excellent source for those with problem feet.

Boot Care

Proper care of your footwear begins with the breaking in of the new boots. No matter how perfect the fit, all new boots will require a certain amount of breaking in before using them on your first extended hike. However, don't expect the breaking-in process to correct a poorly fitted boot.

While a great deal of misinformation concerning boot break in has been passed down by various "experts," the process is really very simple. Put on the socks you expect to wear while hiking, lace on the boots, and go for a walk. Or, rather, go for a series of short walks, gradually increasing the length of time you wear the boots until they feel perfectly comfortable. During the breaking-in process, be especially careful of blisters and sore spots, and stop your walk as soon as any discomfort is felt. A week or so of taking long evening walks should be sufficient to break in all but the very stiffest hiking boot.

The oft-quoted method of standing in a tub of hot water while wearing your new boots and then wearing them around the house until they are dry is frowned upon by virtually all boot manufacturers and should never be used. No boot should require such drastic treatment, and this procedure can ruin a good boot before it is ever used for its intended purpose. Occasionally, though, with a very stiff boot, it may be helpful to soak your heavy socks in water, and then wring them out until they are only slightly damp before wearing the boot. This will help the boot to form to your feet, and will not damage the leather.

Never, never put on a new pair of boots and take off on an extended backpacking trip. No matter how comfortable the boots feel, they will require at least a minimal breaking-in period. The surest route to foot problems is the wearing of brand-new boots on the trail. Don't expect to grit your teeth and bear it until they are broken in. Many an otherwise promising trip has been ruined and aborted by inexperienced hikers attempting to do just that.

Following the breaking-in period and throughout the remainder of their life, boots require a minimal amount of care but that care is very important, and can greatly prolong the life of the boot. Routine boot care is aimed at eliminating problems caused by the two major enemies of leather—water and excessive heat. The boots must be regularly treated to prevent them from absorbing moisture, and they must not be subjected to high temperatures.

A variety of waterproofing agents exist, and each has its advocates. Basically, boot dressings will be either silicone, oil, or wax types, or a combination of these. Some authorities suggest using an oil-type dressing on oil-tanned leathers and a silicone-type dressing on chrome-tanned boots. However, oil-based dressings tend to soften the leather, and allow the boot to stretch excessively, so others suggest avoiding the oil-type treatments altogether.

The method that has worked well for me involves the use of two products—Sno-Seal, a wax/silicone combination, and Leath-R-Seal, a shellac/wax combination. Prior to their first use, and whenever needed thereafter, the boot uppers should be treated by rubbing them thoroughly with Sno-Seal and then warming them *very gently* over a heat source. The heat should only melt the wax and allow it to soak into the leather, and should never cause the boot to become hot to the touch. Never place your boots in the oven for this purpose as even a very low setting can break down the cements used in their construction, and can dry out the leather. As the wax melts, rub it in well, and continue applying more until the boot is essentially saturated. Then, using the dauber that is supplied, spread a coat of Leath-R-Seal around the welt and the boot seams. Allow the boots to dry overnight before using.

The solvents and carriers used with most silicone products (especially the aerosol types) and most oils can often dissolve the glues used in the sole construction of the boot, and you should not let these products contact the welt or sole area. The Sno-Seal/Leath-R-Seal combination avoids this problem and can form the basis of sound boot care.

Perhaps more boots have been ruined by attempting to dry them too quickly over excessive heat or by simply trying to warm your feet around a campfire or stove than by any other means. Unfortunately, there is no way to dry boots quickly and safely. And, though it feels good and looks picturesque to sit with your feet propped up on a rock by the fire, it's death on boots and fine leather. Don't do it!

If your boots have become muddy and soaked with water, don't allow them to dry before scraping them off, as the drying mud will completely dehydrate the leather and will lead to cracking and premature aging. Rapid heating from a stove or fire will lead to the same problem. Instead, wipe off the wet boots as completely as possible, even washing them off if necessary. Dry the outside of the boot as thoroughly as possible with a cloth and stuff them with crumpled newspaper to absorb water from inside. Then allow the leather to dry naturally at room temperature. The wet newspaper can be replaced after several hours. When the boots are dry, immediately re-treat them with the Sno-Seal/Leath-R-Seal combination.

It is usually a good practice to clean and re-treat your boots at the end of every trip, and many hikers like to store their boots with boot trees inside. This is a good practice to prevent them from curling at the toes. If you do this, though, be sure to use wooden or plastic trees rather than metal ones that can rust and damage the inside of the boot. In the off-season, the boots can be "greased" and placed in plastic bags for storage.

With a minimum amount of loving care, a good pair of hiking boots will last many years and will carry you over literally thousands of miles of trails. You owe it to them and yourself to treat your boots kindly.

2

Clothing
by Clifford L. Jacobson

The usual advice given to new backpackers is to scrounge suitable outdoor clothing from home. "Don't buy anything," you are advised, "until you are sure you like the sport." On the surface this advice appears sound, especially if your excursions will be limited to day trips on well-traveled trails. While it's pretty obvious that you need the right gear for extended outings, it's easy to pass over the importance of being suitably clothed and equipped for a short jaunt in the woods. This is because short hikes give you a false sense of security. "So what if a storm blows up," you think. "I'm only 3 miles from the car and I can easily cover that distance in an hour."

Statistically, it can be shown that most serious injuries—from broken legs to hypothermia—occur within a few miles of civilization. Experienced wilderness packers seldom have problems. They are suitably equipped and they are very careful. If you have to cover a 3-mile distance to your car in a driving hailstorm while dressed in just a T-shirt, shorts, and sneakers, you will at best become severely chilled; at worst, you will die from overexposure. Woodsmanship is also important, of course, but without the right gear you may be in for a miserable experience should you encounter difficult weather conditions.

You need very little in the way of outdoor clothing, but essential items must be carefully selected. With discretion you can adapt some cast-off items of clothing from home and you can save money by purchasing garments from secondhand and military surplus stores. When choosing clothing and equipment for backpacking, consider the following criteria:

(1) Is it lightweight? A 45-pound pack feels much differently than a 35-pound one. Ten pounds doesn't seem like much, until you have to carry them and are half way through the ascent of your second hill. Your first strenuous backpacking trip will convince you to leave everything but the necessities at home, and you will quickly learn to pare those necessities down to those that are *absolutely* necessary.

(2) Is it compact? When you have filled your pack with food, cooking gear, stove, gasoline, and tent, there will be little room left for additional baggage. It is essential then that you select clothing that can be rolled or stuffed compactly so it will take up little room.

(3) Will it serve more than one purpose? A single parka, for example, should provide both wind and rain protection. A wool shirt should be large enough to be worn as a jacket over other layers of clothing. A hat should keep your head warm, shade the sun, and provide protection from rain. Under average hiking conditions, you just can't afford the weight and bulk of two similar garments or items of equipment.

Fabrics

Wool. Despite the widespread use of synthetic fabrics, pure, soft wool is still best for keeping you warm. Strands of woven wool intertwine, knot, and intertwine again, to produce a fabric that is wonderfully efficient for trapping heat. Best of all, wool does not absorb water the way other materials do. When wet, wool retains most of its thermal efficiency and always feels warm against the skin. On those chilly, misty mornings when the dampness has caused the down in your vest to lump and your cotton shirt and pants are wet and clammy from clinging moisture, you can put on your wool garments, right next to the skin—scratchy or not—and be grateful for their warmth and for your good sense in bringing them along.

Wet or damp, even the best polyesters, like duPont's Dacron Fiberfill II and Celanese Fortrel PolarGuard, take a back seat to wool. For this reason, no serious backpacker will take to the trails without one upper garment of at least 85 percent wool. But there are drawbacks.

Wool tends to be heavy and good quality shirts and sweaters are very expensive.

Also, wool is not very windproof. Anyone who has ever stood on a windswept ski slope and felt the chill penetrate an unprotected wool ski sweater has realized the value of a cotton or nylon wind covering.

Tight knit woolens provide better wind protection than looser knit ones, are more compact, and tend to snag less easily in brushy areas. Loose knit woolens are warmer and lighter. Consequently, many experienced backpackers prefer a hand-knit (or loose machine-knit) sweater for warmth and wet-weather protection, but they cover this sweater with a nylon or cotton parka.

Cotton. Closely woven cotton is a wonderful fabric for use in parkas and overshirts. Being a natural material, cotton fibers swell when they soak up water. This expansion seals the small openings in the fabric and makes the cloth moderately water repellent. If a tightly woven cotton parka is worn over a wool shirt, you will be quite comfortable in a light rain. In time, of course, the cotton will soak through and the wool will become wet. But unless the rain is very cold, such a combination will probably keep you more comfortable than confining rain gear.

Cotton is sometimes blended with nylon for strength. One of the most popular blends is 60/40 storm cloth that consists of nylon threads woven in the warp direction and cotton threads woven in the fill direction. The result is a marvelously strong, highly windproof garment that possesses moderate water repellency. Sixty/forty parkas have become quite popular in recent years. They are practical garments, light in weight, and many are stylish enough for in-town use.

Cotton has also been successfully blended with Dacron polyester in a 65 percent cotton, 35 percent Dacron ratio. Most important, however, is the fact that 65/35 fabrics are a bidirectional weave, or an "intimate blend" as it is called in the industry. This means that both the cotton and the Dacron are first blended together as individual strands. The blended strands are then woven to form the fabric. The advantage of 65/35 material becomes obvious the first time you wear an outer garment of this fabric in a rain. The cotton/Dacron cloth is much more water repellent than 60/40, though it is no more wind or snag proof. Sixty-five/thirty-five fabric accepts water-repellent compounds much better than 60/40 (nylon won't absorb the compound), and one of these parkas treated with a good water-repellent spray will remain nearly impervious to water in a heavy downpour for 20 minutes or more.

APPALACHIAN PARKA

Blended fabrics are ideal for outerwear. In 65/35 storm cloth the fabric is made of 65 percent cotton and 35 percent Dacron polyester. The strands of each are first blended together to form one strand and then the combination is woven to form the fabric. The result is a fabric that is windproof and highly water repellent.

Poplin is any tightly woven cotton. Today's better "canvas" tents are not canvas, but are a specially treated, lightweight cotton poplin.

Ventile is tightly woven cotton poplin. It was developed in England during World War II to keep downed British fliers from freezing. Ventile cotton parkas are amazingly watertight and are breathable (that is, they dispel body moisture). Unfortunately, ventile cloth is very expensive and heavy. An average parka weighs around 3 pounds, which is much too heavy for average backpacking conditions. These garments are also somewhat bulky.

If you do a good deal of hiking at high altitudes where wind-driven snow and hail is a frequent occurrence, then a heavy-duty parka of cotton or blended cotton may be a wise investment. But if you are put off by the $45 or more cost of one of these parkas, an inexpensive military surplus field jacket will serve just as well. Field jackets are really true double-shell mountain parkas and the newer models come with Velcro-fastened cuffs and permanently attached hoods that are hidden within a zippered compartment in the collar. Tailoring and construction is of the highest quality and these parkas, which can generally be purchased for under $20, will give you years of good service. If the olive drab color offends you, bleach out the color and dye the fabric to suit your taste. I have a fine army field jacket that has been dyed vivid red. It has attracted many complimentary glances on the hiking trails and performs just as well in wind and snow as its much more expensive relatives.

Nylon. Nylon is the most successful fabric for use in backpacking equipment. Everything from shirts to rain gear to tents, and even boots is now offered in this wonder material. There is no doubt that nylon has made the backpacker's journeys more comfortable and safer.

Nylon garments are available in both taffeta and rip-stop weaves. The difference between the two fabrics is immediately obvious. Taffeta has a continuous weave while rip-stop has slightly thicker thread woven in at regular intervals. The thicker threads run in both warp and fill directions and discourage tearing. Because the rip-stop grid patterns occur about each quarter inch or so, weight is kept to a minimum; hence, the lightest of these fabrics may run only about 1.1 ounces per square yard.

Both single- and double-ply high-count taffetas are claimed by many manufacturers to be more abrasion resistant and puncture proof than lower-count, rip-stop fabrics. Nevertheless, rip-stop often outsells taffeta because it is lighter, less expensive, and classier looking. In use, there

is probably very little difference between the two fabrics if equivalent
weights of material are compared. However, experienced backpackers
are in agreement that any nylon fabric—rip-stop or taffeta—that weighs
less than 1.9 ounces per square yard is too light for outer garments.
Very lightweight nylon tends to snag and tear easily—an important
consideration if your hikes will take you through brushy areas.

Waterproofing Nylon. Nylon does not expand and become water
repellent when it gets wet so it must be coated with plastic to make it
waterproof. The type and thickness of the plastic (usually polyurethane) coating vary and depend upon the purpose for which the
garment will be used. For example, a fabric that must be highly waterproof is usually given several light coats of polyurethane. The water-
proofness of this coating can be measured by the manufacturer with a
test that simply consists of forcing water through the fabric under
pressure. The thicker the plastic coating, the greater pressure it will
withstand. A fabric that will tolerate 100 pounds or more of water per
square inch on this test is obviously more durable—and more expensive—than the lighter variety that will accept between 0 and 50 pounds
of water per square inch. For this reason, you should beware of inexpensive foreign copies of quality-coated American garments. These
may look serviceable in the store but may absorb water like a sponge
in the first heavy rain. This is not to say that imported nylon fabrics
are bad; some are excellent, but it is not easy to tell the quality of the
coating by looking at or handling the fabric. However, you can perform a simple test by pouring a small amount of water onto the material. Rub the water well into the fabric with your hand (this will
simulate a pressure test), then pour it off. Repeat the test, only this
time allow the water to "stand" for a few minutes before pouring it
off. Does the water bead up or does it leave a damp spot? It should not
be possible to force water by hand through a properly waterproofed
garment.

Outerwear

You may begin a hike in the early morning hours when the temperature is in the 40s. By noon, the thermometer may read a sweltering 90,
and by later afternoon it may drop into the more comfortable 70s.
During the course of the day you may experience a short warm rain, a

long wind-driven hailstorm, and at high altitudes, snow. All of which means your outerwear must be versatile, warm, and quickly changeable.

Shirts and Sweaters

It is common knowledge that many light layers of clothing are warmer and more versatile than a single heavy coat or sweater, so your wardrobe will be most adaptable if you include one lightweight wool shirt and one mediumweight wool jac-shirt or sweater. A very light, coated nylon parka that weighs only 2 to 3 ounces will complete the protection against chill and rain. Where colder weather is expected, an additional light wool shirt or possibly a down or polyester vest may be added.

As you hike you will continually adjust your wardrobe, so choose shirts and sweaters that button down the front rather than those that pull over the head. A light, over-the-head stretchy sweater is fine, but a machine woven, slipover wool shirt that has no stretch or give can be a real nuisance. You can find good buys on high-quality wool shirts at your local military surplus store. Granted, such shirts are not as attractive as the expensive, well-tailored models found in equipment shops, but they are just as serviceable. You may not be the envy of the backpacking crowd if you adorn yourself from head to toe in olive drab, but you will be just as comfortable, and for a whole lot less money.

Down-Filled Outerwear

Vests and lightweight jackets filled with duck or goose down are very popular among backpackers, and for good reason. Down provides more warmth for its weight than any other material, and clothing filled with down stuffs into the smallest of spaces. Nevertheless, most down garments may be too warm for average backpacking conditions. A light vest, worn over a mediumweight wool shirt, and covered with a cotton or nylon wind shell, offers protection from cold down into the low 20s. Unless you will be tripping in the winter or at high altitudes, any down-filled garment more substantial than a vest, or at most a sweater (a vest with sleeves), will be much too warm and is just needless bulk on the trail.

The quality of down depends upon the climate in which the ducks or geese are raised. Down that is imported from Asian or South American countries often tends to be of poorer quality than that from birds raised in a colder, more demanding environment. Such low-quality down may keep you warm under most conditions but it lacks the stam-

DOWN VEST

The down vest is becoming more and more popular, even outside the back-packing world. Stuffed with insulating material, it will keep your body warm and your arms free. A light vest worn over a mediumweight wool shirt and then covered with a cotton or nylon windbreaker can offer warmth down into the low 20s.

ina and resilience of down from heartier climates. At the first washing or cleaning, inferior down may turn to string. At best, it will never regain its original loft.

Manufacturers are quick to point out that goose down is better than duck down. If you're in the market for a down sleeping bag, you may want to purchase the best down you can find. This is because a down bag has baffled tubes and the down within each tube is free to loft fully, to produce the greatest thickness and thus the greatest warmth. But when buying outerwear, the difference between duck and goose down is less important, because down-filled garments, with a few rare exceptions, are not baffled. Rather, the down is quilted into squares or bands and hence is under some compression. Thus, regardless of the type of down used in a vest or jacket, its loft is restricted, so you gain only a very slight advantage by using the highest quality down. (A complete discussion of down is given in Chapter 4.)

Because down retains almost no thermal efficiency when wet, it has lost favor among backpackers. The trend in outergarments is back to wool, or for cold weather, to one of the new synthetics like PolarGuard or Dacron Fiberfill II. A Fiberfill II or PolarGuard vest, jacket, or parka, for example, will provide warmth equivalent to a similar down-filled garment, but it will weigh only an ounce or two more and be only slightly less compact when stuffed into its carrying sack. Unlike down, PolarGuard and Dacron II absorb very little water when they are wet, so they can be wrung out and worn immediately, and still keep you warm. Outerwear is much more apt to get wet than a carefully cared for sleeping bag, so the choice should be obvious. Choose down outerwear only when you are sure you won't get it wet. For most of us the synthetics are best. They are more rugged, easier to care for, more reliable in wet weather, and far less expensive than the natural product.

Pants

For warm weather cotton pants are fine, but for cold, wet conditions and for use at high altitudes, the choice again is wool. A major consideration when buying pants is to make sure they are unrestrictive—baggy, if you will—to provide ample room for raising your legs high, as when ascending a steep slope. Military surplus fatigues or field pants serve admirably in this respect and are very inexpensive—generally around $5 a pair. For colder weather, get the mediumweight officer's model wool pants (about $10 a pair), and for snow hiking, select the heavier, buff-colored GI pants. Cut off or hem the bottoms (don't cuff

For cold, wet conditions woolen pants are the choice. Whether they're cut long or are knicker-types, they should be unrestrictive or perhaps even baggy, so that they'll give you ample room for climbing and walking.

them) so they hang about one inch below your boot tops. Pants that are too long catch on brush and sop up mud and water.

For short trips an extra pair of sturdy long pants is permissible, but for long trips they are just excess baggage. At $5 to $10 a pair you can afford to begin a backpacking trip with a sturdy new pair of army fatigues that, in strenuous use, should last at least a month.

Shorts

Many experienced hikers prefer to wear shorts. There are even a few hearty packers who wear them for cross-country skiing. I must admit that I have never been a fan of short pants. They leave my legs sunburned, brush bruised, and mosquito bitten. But if you like shorts, just make sure you get them with plenty of room in the legs so you can move freely.

Rain Gear

Backpackers are not in complete agreement as to what constitutes the best rain gear. Many hikers like an oversized poncho that covers both their body and the pack. Other walkers wear only a urethane-coated nylon rain jacket and let their legs get wet. Still other packers prefer the mountain climber's cagoule, which is simply a modified below-the-knee fisherman's rain shirt. Sturdy nylon rain parkas are popular and so are rain chaps. Most hikers consider rain pants just extra weight because their legs get soaked anyway from the trapped perspiration. On the other hand, those who hike in the wet, brushy rain forests along the Oregon and Washington coast think rain pants, or at least chaps, are a necessity.

Wearing rain gear while carrying a backpack poses some problems, not the least of which is what to do with the pack's padded hip belt. The friction generated by a tight hip belt against a coated nylon garment will abrade the waterproof coating of the fabric in short order. So will the pressure from the pack's shoulder straps. Consequently, if you do a lot of wet-weather backpacking, you might want to consider a more substantial kind of rain gear than lightweight coated nylon. The rubberized rain suits that are popular with West Coast loggers are very adequate, although they are somewhat heavy. A lighter and less expensive solution is an oversized poncho that is designed to cover both hiker and pack. Ponchos are not subject to the abrasion of belts because they are put on over the pack. On the negative side, ponchos flap in the wind unmercifully and thus do a poor job of keeping you dry. However, they are liked by many backpackers because they can be used as a ground cloth for tentless camping or as extra protection inside a tent in the event the floor should leak. But you should be wary about using your rain gear as a ground cloth. Regardless of the care you take, small holes and abrasions will begin to appear in the fabric and your poncho will leak profusely the next time it is called upon to serve its primary function.

Possibly the best choice for the occasional wet-weather hiker is a lightweight, heavily coated, nylon rain parka. The parka should have a full zippered front for good ventilation and a hood for foul weather. Velcro-fasteners or snap closures at the wrist provide better temperature control than elastic wristlets, because the looser the fit the easier it will be for body moisture to escape.

One of the most versatile garments is the oversized rain poncho. This model is made to cover not only the backpacker but his backpack as well. It can also serve as a ground cloth or even a shelter if need be.

If you do backpack in the rain, I would advise against buying expensive rain gear, for pack straps and hip belts, as mentioned, will ruin the material. Additionally, the increased weight and bulk of pockets, zipper overflaps, ventilated panels, and other niceties merely add to the weight and bulk of the rain gear, which is a disadvantage when you try to stuff it into an already overweight and overcrowded backpack. Then, too, you may pay for accessories that you don't really need. For example, a ventilated back panel that eliminates perspiration is a worthwhile investment if you hike packless in the rain, but the vent won't function if you cover it with a pack. Pockets are a needless expense because the straps and belts of the backpack make their use awkward. Other features, such as zippered legs in rain pants, may be a downright nuisance, especially when you try to operate them when the pants are caked with mud and debris. And those extra cost snaps or Velcro closures at the ankle of rain pants serve little purpose other than to restrict ventilation. It is best to trim rain pants about an inch longer than your hiking pants and let them hang loose so the air will be pumped in and out with each step.

Headwear
Because your brain receives about one-fifth of your body's blood supply, a sizable amount of heat is stored in your head. Jacques Cos-

Many hikers never even give a thought to head gear. But because so much of your body's heat is lost through the top of the head, you should always make sure you've got it adequately covered in cold weather. The rule should be serviceability rather than fashionability.

teau once commented that if his divers removed their rubberized skull caps while working beneath the polar ice sheet, they would quickly die from exposure to the icy water, even though the rest of their body remained well protected by the special neoprene suits they wore.

Many hikers just don't give enough thought to a hat. Though properly clothed, they rely entirely on the hood of their parkas to protect their heads. Hoods are adequate for warm weather, but where a wide range of climatic conditions may be encountered, a hat of some sort is essential. For cool weather, this means a wool stocking cap or beret, and for summer hiking, a crushable hat of wool felt or cotton/Dacron sailcloth. While hat styles, weaves, fabrics, and construction make for interesting conversation, you will probably end up choosing a head covering that flatters your personality. If how you look is important to you, choose your hat accordingly, but remember that the model you select should provide adequate protection. This may mean carrying an extra, less-flattering hat in your pack.

When the temperature drops below freezing, mittens of some sort are a must. If they're made out of wool, so much the better, since they'll keep your hands warm even if they get wet. For the cold-hands type there are even down-covered mittens.

Gloves

The first time you encounter a spell of cold, penetrating rain, you will wish you had brought along a pair of gloves. In an emergency, you can wear a pair of wool hiking socks over your hands. But a pair of lightweight, leather deerskin gloves is the best solution and is equally handy for performing a variety of camp chores. For spring and fall hiking, leather-faced, all-wool gloves are a better choice, since wool retains a great deal of warmth when wet. When temperatures are generally below freezing, mittens of some sort are a must. Though gloves are seemingly an insignificant item and thus are often overlooked by backpackers, they will pay for themselves in comfort on the first raw, windy day.

Although not an item of clothing, an important companion to gloves is hand lotion. A small amount of good quality lotion rubbed well into your hands will not only prevent chapping but will seal the pores of the skin and extend the low end of the temperature range at which your hands will be comfortable. This is the reason why swimmers "grease" their bodies before engaging in a long cold swim.

Parkas

The primary function of a parka is to provide wind and water protection. Warmth is attained by the layered clothing worn beneath the parka. Parkas range in style from inexpensive, compact nylon affairs, like those used for bicycling, to impeccably constructed double- and triple-layered jackets designed for use by mountaineers in extreme conditions.

Most backpackers do not need the heavy, bulky parkas of the mountaineer. For average use, where weight should be kept to a minimum, a simple hooded rain jacket will suffice to break both wind and rain. If the rain parka is somewhat on the baggy side, it will usually flap sufficiently in the wind to eliminate body perspiration.

Although manufacturers have tried to produce a single parka that will shed rain yet eliminate body moisture, a garment that will do both efficiently does not exist. If you choose to carry a poncho for rain protection, then a nonwaterproof windshell may be the perfect companion. But if you choose to travel as light and compact as possible, then a lightweight coated rain parka will have to perform both functions. To eliminate the abrasion of the hip belt against the coated fabric, push the back of the parka above the hip belt and secure the belt below the parka. At least one manufacturer (Kelty) has given some thought to this problem and has provided a method of running the hip belt through the pocket slits within the parka.

Underwear

For greatest comfort, the choice rests between cotton and wool. Nylon underwear is liked by some, though it has a clammy feel when it becomes damp from perspiration. On the plus side, nylon undergarments dry much faster than cotton and are lighter and more compact.

Perhaps the best underwear for serious backpacking is the fishnet or string type that consists of a gridwork of woven cotton or wool. When a tightly buttoned shirt or jacket is worn over the net, a large volume of air becomes trapped in the weave, and it is this dead air that keeps you warm. When the overshirt is unbuttoned, however, trapped air (and perspiration) is released and your body is cooled rapidly. Fishnet underwear is so successful for keeping you warm—or cool—that for a short time after its development during World War II, it was kept a military secret. In addition to providing excellent temperature control, net underwear is very light and thus is well liked by hikers. A few manufacturers are now using wool to make this versatile underwear.

Backpackers who dislike net longies complain that the sustained pressure of the pack straps imprints a wafflelike pattern in their skin. This problem is easily remedied, however, by choosing fishnet underwear with a solid panel of material over the yoke. Most equipment shops stock this special underwear.

For cold, wet conditions, experienced hikers still select underwear with a high wool content, and Grandpa's itchy-scratchy long johns can't be beat. Unfortunately, wool underwear is very expensive and military surplus, while an acceptable second choice, is only about 50 percent wool. Some hikers omit long johns in cold weather and instead wear a soft wool or cashmere sweater next to the skin. These sweaters, which were popular in the 1950s, can often be found for next to noth-

Either cotton or wool underwear will give you the greatest comfort, whether in a tight weave or in the fishnet style. For cold, wet conditions underwear with high wool content will serve well. But no matter which you choose, wool or cotton, you should wear some kind of long john if you're venturing out in the cold.

ing at second-hand stores and garage sales. For very cold weather, where long underpants are essential, you can keep the cost down by purchasing army surplus officers' summer wool pants (the sand-colored, very light wool models). To save weight and bulk, rip out the pockets and install a corded waistband. Shrink the pants in hot water until they fit.

For average summer backpacking conditions though, you don't need long johns. Unless you will be hiking in wet, cold, or very unpredictable climates, you can get by wearing whatever you wear at home. An extra set of underwear is sufficient for long trips, and for short trips no change is necessary.

Socks

Like the infantry, the backpacker travels on his feet. Those good boots you bought will blister your feet raw without proper cushioning, and high-quality socks provide the padding. For greatest comfort and to minimize friction, most hikers wear two pairs of socks—a very sheer ankle-high pair and a higher, medium-weight pair. A few tough-footed packers get by with only a single pair of mediumweight or heavyweight socks. There seems to be no set rule on the number and kind of socks to wear. Most hikers experiment and choose what is most comfortable. Experienced hikers do, however, insist that socks have a high wool content—at least 85 percent. Wool absorbs moisture better than other materials and compresses less when it is wet. On those damp, rainy days, where every step takes you through a mud hole, you will appreciate the warmth of wool.

Hikers who are allergic to wool can wear an inner sock of nylon, cotton, or silk. Socks of sheer silk are available from shops that handle cross-country ski equipment. They are wonderfully comfortable, extremely warm, but incredibly expensive.

For an extended hiking trip you need at least two and preferably three pairs of good wool socks. These socks tend to be expensive—approximately $3 to $7 a pair—so if you are on a budget visit your military surplus store. The standard army hiking sock is very inexpensive, and for summer use is an acceptable alternative to the more expensive quality woolens.

The trend today is toward boots with 6- to 7-inch tops, so sock height should reflect this trend. Socks with 12- to 24-inch tops are fine for use with knickers but they ride down the calf, bulk up, and become uncomfortable after a short time. Besides, why pay for the extra length if you don't need it?

A major problem on backpacking trips is washing your socks. Bulky wool socks take a long time to dry, even when they're tied to your packframe and exposed to the sun on a hot, windy day. One solution to this problem is to wash and wring dry only the sheer liner socks and to hang these on the packframe to dry. The heavier outer socks can be tied to the frame unwashed where they will air dry and be "purified" by the sun.

Another common method of drying socks is to wear them to bed. However, this is very uncomfortable and merely transfers the water from your socks to your sleeping bag. If you use this method you'll wake up in the morning with a damp sleeping bag that must be dried in the same manner as your socks—slowly, by exposure to the sun.

Gaiters

Gaiters consist of a sleeve of material that attaches beneath the instep of your boot and extends well above the boot top. They serve to keep snow, grass, sticks, and other debris out of your boots, and are commonly available in lengths from about 7 inches to 16 or more inches in cotton, nylon, or blended materials. Attachment to the boots is with zippers, snaps, or laces.

Summer hikers have little use for gaiters, though winter and mountain travelers will find them useful for reducing the intake of snow in their boots. When purchasing gaiters, it is important to consider the type of material used and the method of attachment to the boots. Experienced hikers generally prefer a breathable, water-repellent fabric to one that is completely watertight. And a lace or snap attachment is usually selected because zippers can freeze or jam and are difficult to adjust while wearing gloves. An easy running nylon zipper, if covered with a protective overlap, is well liked by many winter hikers. The height of gaiters is a personal choice, but high top models are most effective in eliminating unwanted debris.

The value of suitable clothing, even for a short trip, should not be taken lightly, as the experience of 27-year-old Stephen Collier illustrates. On Thanksgiving day, 1974, Stephen and his friend, Patrick Eagan, set out to hike a portion of the High Peaks area of the Adirondack Mountains in New York State. The temperature was in the low 20s. This was Steve's first backpacking trip and he wore blue jeans, cotton long johns, and a cotton flannel shirt. Pat wore similar attire except for corduroy knickers. The first day was uneventful and the pair easily made the journey to a trailside lean-to where they spent the night.

The second day dawned clear and bright, though there was some snow on the ground and a hint of more to come. Pat led the way up the tortuous mountain trail and Steve followed. When it began to snow, climbing became strenuous and Steve's pace became slower, his footsteps less sure. He began to stumble and he fell frequently. Somewhere along the trail he lost his hat. Pat now realized that Steve was in trouble so he decided to seek help at a ranger station about half a mile away. Steve, who could no longer walk, sat down by the trail to wait and Pat covered him with a down jacket that he pulled from his pack. Quickly, Pat scurried down the snow-covered trail and about two hours later he returned with help. Unfortunately, it was too late. Steve's body core temperature had already dropped into the low 80s. He was in the last stages of hypothermia (overexposure) and he died shortly thereafter.

Information about what to wear and take on a hiking trip is readily available in every good backpacking book. For this reason, even the most inexperienced hiker should be adequately prepared when he takes to the trails.

3

Packs and Frames

by Don Geary

The second most important piece of backpacking equipment (next to boots) is your pack. Into it will go all of your worldly possessions while on the trail: food, clothing, cooking gear, tent, and sleeping bag. Thus it is obviously of considerable importance that you choose your backpack with the greatest care.

There are at least 40 manufacturers producing over 50 different selections of packbags and frames. Prices range from around $20 for cheapies to more than $100 for expedition-type models. With so many different styles being offered for sale, how do you go about choosing the right backpack?

The best way to begin narrowing down the field is to decide what type of hiking you expect to do. There are three broad categories of hikers: day hikers, overnighters (one or two nights on the trail), and longer than three-day hikers.

Packs for dayhikers are simple, small, and lightweight. No frame is needed because the load will usually not exceed 10 pounds. Day packs usually contain a camera, film, lunch, and possibly a sweater. Obviously, if you are not going to be on the trail overnight you can eliminate a lot of gear. Some type of day pack is produced by every one of the major equipment manufacturers and they are all basically the same—a small, teardrop-shaped bag, sometimes with either an outside pocket or

This day pack is made of waterproof nylon duck and has a chrome-tanned leather bottom to provide strength against abrasion. It's priced at around $20 and is ideal for one-day hikes into the wilderness.

an internal compartment. Some day packs have leather bottoms (to withstand rock climbing abuse) and accessory straps for attaching such things as ice axes and camera tripods to the pack. Prices for the standard day pack start at about $10 and go up to $30 for the leather-bottomed models.

A day pack can also be a fanny or belt pack. Fanny packs are simply small, long packs that are attached to a belt and worn around the waist. They are great for short hikes when only a few items—lunch and a sweater, for example—are carried. Prices range from $10 to $20.

The most popular backpacks are those designed to carry enough gear for one or two nights on the trail. Packs of this type are for loads of approximately 30 pounds and do not necessarily have a frame. Frameless packs are usually called rucksacks and are popular with climbers because the load is carried low and close to the back. Most of the weight is carried by the shoulders and not on the hips as with conventional frame packs.

Rucksacks, which have become popular with trail hikers over the past ten years, have initiated a good deal of research and development.

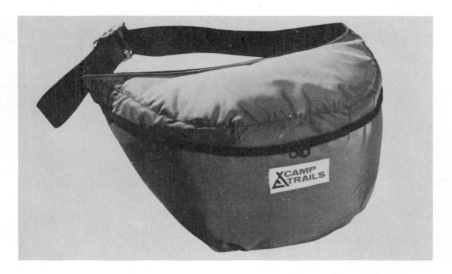

For carrying a small number of items, such as on a short day hike, the fanny pack is most useful. Worn around the waist, it leaves the arms and shoulders free for picture taking, fishing, or just balance.

The first rucksacks were developed during World War II to help American GIs carry heavy loads. These heavy-duty rucksacks had a tubular aluminum frame with a shape that remotely resembles an inverted letter T. The bag was made of heavy cotton duck or canvas with four to six outside pockets and several straps for pulling the load (whether great or small) closer to the frame, thereby eliminating any sloppiness. The old GI rucksacks were heavy but once you got the load up on your back you could carry it for long periods. These old World War II rucksacks are still available in Army and Navy surplus stores for around $20.

During the Vietnam war the U.S. Marines developed a lighter version of the World War II rucksack. The bag was made from tough nylon and there was an internal X-type frame that was semiflexible. This frame was sewn on the back of the pack and the straps were attached here. Unfortunately, I have never seen this type of rucksack for sale in this country.

Recreational Equipment, Inc. (REI), in Seattle, offers a line of rucksacks from France that are simple and first class. The French line is called *Sacs Millet* and prices range from $30 to $40. These packs are what I call true rucksacks because they are simply a bag with no frame. Almost all of the weight of the load is carried by the shoulders.

Several American manufacturers now produce variations of the

The Eiger Standard, from Alpine Designs, is an example of an internal frame pack. The aluminum frame bends to fit the contour of the back. It's larger than a day pack, but, of course, smaller than a pack designed for use with a frame.

standard rucksack and these packs are ideal for one- or two-day hikes. Kelty, for example, makes a rucksack with a capacity of up to 2,800 cubic inches. Alpine Designs makes the Eiger Standard, a good rucksack with a capacity of 2,000 cubic inches. Sierra Designs makes the Summit pack along similar lines. All are ideal for up to two-day hikes.

Even more popular than the rucksack for up to two-day hikes is the frame pack. There are, undoubtedly, more than 50 different models, styles, and manufacturers. Backpacking has become a very popular form of recreation and has resulted in everybody and his brother trying to make a buck off unsuspecting equipment buyers. This is the main reason that you will see frame packs for sale in every sporting goods discount house from Boston to Bakersfield. It is possible to buy a frame pack for less than $20 that *looks* just about the same as a frame pack that sells for $125. And you can bet that the cheapies outsell the expensive numbers by about ten to one, regardless of the fact that the more expensive models will outlast the cheapies by 100 to 1. A classic case of false economy.

I see it this way: A person who has never gone backpacking decides to give hiking a try. There are a number of things this uninitiated hiker has read about, which he feels are necessary for a stay in the wilderness. A down sleeping bag ($60 to $100), boots ($50), tent ($100 plus), and a pack to carry the stuff. What usually happens is that our would-be hiker buys a $20 sleeping bag, $20 tent, $20 pair of "hiking" boots, and a $20 frame pack, plus other "needed" items. This amounts to an investment of around $100 in bad equipment for a shot at hiking for the first time. The results are predictable: The poor fellow goes on his first trip, gets blisters from bad boots, spends a night shivering in an inadequate sleeping bag inside a leaking tent, and has his pack fall apart on the first day out. But afterwards, none of that matters, because the guy will never set foot in the woods again. Hiking is for masochists, he says, not for him. He considers the $100 a bad investment, is happy he didn't spend $300, and usually winds up giving the gear to his kid brother.

It is possible that if he had spent a bit more time choosing his gear and just a few more dollars all around, this new hiker might have gotten a better idea of what backpacking is all about. Common sense plays an important role in choosing equipment for the trail, and so does a basic understanding of the differences between quality and shoddy equipment.

One way to avoid a bad equipment investment, which inevitably results in a very strong dislike for hiking, is to rent equipment before buying. Obviously, it will not be possible to rent equipment in all areas of the country, but if you live near a large city or if there is a quality equipment shop in your area, chances are good that you will be able to rent what you need for your first few trips out. This makes a lot of sense. You get a chance to experience backpacking without a large outlay of cash and can decide whether or not you care to invest in equipment. Another advantage of renting equipment is that you can try several types of backpacks before reaching a final purchase decision.

A second way to avoid a bad equipment investment is to borrow equipment from friends. Most people who are into backpacking have extra gear. Ask around and you should be able to borrow enough equipment for an overnight hike.

Another possibility is to buy used equipment. Backpacking shops that specialize in quality equipment often sell used equipment that has been traded in. It is often possible to buy a used backpack for half the new price, so it may be to your advantage to inquire at your local equipment shop.

Quality frame packs, as well as other quality backpacking equip-

The most popular bag for extended backpacking is the combination pack and frame. The frame is a tubular aluminum ladderlike unit to which is attached a hip belt to support the load and, of course, a pack. The pack is usually divided into two compartments on the inside and has as many as six pocket attachments.

ment, are not hard to find if you look in the right places. To begin with, you cannot buy a new frame pack that is worth anything for under $30. The range for quality frame packs, in the one- or two-night-out category, is from $30 to $60. A second indication of quality is the name of the maker of the pack. For your first choice, stick with one of the big-name manufacturers listed in the Addenda of this book.

Frame packs are composed of two basic parts: the frame and the pack bag. Frames are made from tubular aluminum and are most commonly welded together, to form a shape that resembles a curved aluminum ladder. Some hikers claim that the only way to make a decent frame is with heliarc welded joints. While it may be true that the weakest parts of a frame are the joints, there are other ways of joining the parts of the frame. Alpine Designs, for example, introduced Lexan couplers a few years ago that joined the pieces of tubular aluminum together. I have been using one of these frames for three years and have never had a problem with the frame.

The pack is usually attached to the frame by a series of clevis pins (three or four on each side of the frame).

The greatest strain on a frame comes when you set your pack down with the weight entirely on one leg of the frame. This is called diagonal stress. When you are shopping for a frame pack you can do a simple test that will indicate how strong the frame is. Stand the pack on the floor and tilt it until it is resting on one leg, then lean on top of the frame putting pressure on the one leg. Increase the pressure until you have an idea of how strong the frame is. Be careful not to exert too much pressure on the frame or you might have to buy a broken one.

Another very important part of a quality frame is the hip belt, for this is where most of the weight will be carried. While the pack itself may be called a "backpack" and the use of the pack may be called "backpacking," the actual load of the pack is carried on the hips.

Hip belts come two ways: one piece and two pieces. The one-piece hip belt is usually padded and is attached to the frame by either clevis pins or some other type of coupling device. The one-piece belt wraps around the hips and fastens with a buckle in the front after the pack is on the back.

Two-piece hip belts work much the same way as one-piece belts except that there is no padding for the small of your back. One piece of the belt is attached to one side of the frame and the other half of the belt is attached to the other side. After the load is up on the back, the belt is tightened.

Above the hip belt on the packframe there is usually some type of back support or webbing that holds the pack away from the back and helps to ventilate the area between the back and the pack. Some makers use one or two 8-inch pieces of nylon mesh as back supports while

The back support system helps keep the pack directly off your back and improves ventilation. These back supports may be in the form of two wide strips of nylon mesh or one full-length web cushion. Both provide adequate ventilation, but the latter helps distribute the pressure of the load evenly across the back.

other makers offer a full-length nylon mesh back support. I prefer the full-length mesh back support because it offers good ventilation while at the same time helping to distribute pressure evenly across the back.

The pack straps or harness of the pack have only one function—to hold the pack in the correct position on your back. Since most of the weight while walking is on the hips, the pack straps do not have to be as strong as you might think. In fact, while standing with a full load on your back, with the hip belt tightened, you should be able to slip a finger under the pack strap where it crosses your shoulder. Straps should be padded, however, and attached to the frame in such a manner as to be adjustable laterally across the top of the crossbar. Straps should also have some type of buckle arrangement so you can make adjustments, allowing for variations in terrain, tired muscles, and slippage.

The second part of the backpacking system is the pack bag and there are a few things that separate the well made from the cheapies. All of the better pack bags are made from waterproof, rip-stop nylon except Kelty. Waterproof, in this case, means that the bag will keep your gear dry in a light drizzle or snow but will leak in a heavy downpour. Kelty recommends that you use a rain cover with its packs.

The way a pack is stitched tells a lot about the workmanship that went into it. All stress points (seams and where zippers are attached) should have at least two rows of stitches. Really strong stitching measures out at ten per inch, but you can get by with a minimum of seven stitches per inch.

If the pack is attached to the frame through grommets, there should be at least three rows of stitching around each grommet hole. Some of the better makers use up to five rows of stitches for these areas.

Most of the better made packs use heavy-duty coil nylon zippers for pockets and compartments. The one exception is Kelty, which uses metal zippers. In cold weather, especially, you should use a pack with nylon zippers because metal has a tendency to freeze.

The pack bag itself should have pockets along both sides. They're handy for such things as a canteen and other frequently used items. Several packs have a map pocket on top of the pack bag, which is convenient but not necessary.

Most pack bags are separated into two sections, a top and a bottom. The top section is the largest and holds the most gear up high, where it belongs. The smaller bottom compartment holds other gear. A two-compartment pack helps you to keep your gear organized and generally makes finding items easier without having to rummage through one large bag.

Pack bags are attached to the frame with either clevis pins through grommetted holes in the bag or are held to the pack frame by frame-coupling devices. Generally speaking, three attachment points per side are sufficient but four are better. Some attachment methods are simple while others require several hands and a little luck to get the bag back onto the frame once it has been removed. Keep in mind that it's only necessary to remove the bag from the frame on rare occasions.

The last classification of backpacks are those that will be used to carry greater loads, for more than three days out in the bush. The basic difference between these types of packs and the one- or two-day packs is that these packs are bigger. Commonly referred to as expedition packs, these units are able to carry loads of 40 to 50 pounds. Probably the biggest advance in large packs has come in the "soft" or rucksack

class. One example worth mentioning is the Jensen Pack, currently
made and sold by the Rivendell Mountain Works in Victor, Idaho.
Some of the noteworthy features of the Jensen Pack are its "S" shape
that conforms to the hiker's back, the slim profile of the loaded pack,
and the superb construction and craftsmanship that goes into the making of the pack.

All of the criteria for judging quality packs apply for the larger
packs as well as the two- to three-day packs. It is possible to buy a
larger pack and use it for short trips most of the time. In the event that
you plan a longer trip, you will at least have the right pack. One drawback of using a larger pack for short hikes is that you tend to take
more equipment than you have to, simply because you have the room.

After you've picked your pack and have packed it according to the
guidelines in Chapter 9, there's one more important question to be
answered before hitting the trail. How do you get the darn thing up
onto your back?

This may not seem very important to you, but if you have never
thrown a pack up onto your back you may be in for a surprise the first
time you give it a try. In fact, it takes a bit of practice to be able to put
a pack on with a little finesse. Probably the easiest way to get a pack
on your back is to have someone else hold the pack in the air while you
slip your arms through the straps. But suppose you want to do this
when no one else is around?

One surefire method is to stand the pack up against a tree or other
fixed object, sit in front of the pack, slip your arms through the straps,
stand up and adjust the pack straps and hip belt.

After a while this method will seem rather silly to you and you will
want to be able to throw the pack up onto your back. There is a simple
trick that will enable you to do this. If you are right-handed, lift your
right knee up and away from your body until it is at about a 90-degree
angle to your hips. Lift your pack up with both hands and balance it
momentarily on your right thigh while at the same time pushing your
right arm through the right pack strap. In the same motion drop your
right leg and turn into the pack while slipping your left arm through
the other pack strap. The whole process takes about two seconds and
is quite fluid. You may find it helpful to lean forward slightly when
you have only one arm in the harness. With a little practice, you
should be able to get your pack on your back in a flash. If you are left-
handed, make the usual adjustments to the right-handed world. When

you take your pack off, lower it gently to the ground or you may do some damage to the frame.

After the pack is on your back, you should tighten the hip belt. Do a kind of half jump to get the pack as high up on your back as possible, and before it slides down pull tightly on the hip belt strap. This usually does the trick. Next, tighten the pack straps enough to bring the load close to your back. As you are walking, especially downhill, you can loosen the hip belt and carry the weight of the pack on your shoulders. After you reach level ground or while going uphill, transfer the weight back to the hips. As you walk, experiment with both the hip belt and pack straps and find the most comfortable combination for you.

Pack Care

Your pack should give you years of service, regardless of how often you take off for the hills. There are a few things that you should do to keep your frame and bag in good shape. First, never set your pack close to an open fire or cook stove—nylon melts. Second, take some care when packing and using your pack. Nylon is tough, but sharp objects will pierce it and abrasive things—such as rocks—will wear holes in the bag. While tubular aluminum with welded joints is a tough combination, rough handling—such as in dropping a loaded pack to the ground—will probably break the frame. Take it from somebody who knows, carrying a broken frame pack is no way to go. When you are camped you should remove all packaged food items from the pack bag in an effort to avoid nocturnal animal damage to the pack and food. A hungry bear can open your pack from the side in just a few seconds.

If your pack gets dirty, you can usually remove the dirt with a damp cloth or sponge. If your pack gets really dirty, you may want to have it dry cleaned. This will do a better job of cleaning the pack and leave your pack looking newer. Check with your local equipment dealer to find a dry cleaner who knows about cleaning nylon. You may also want to have the bag waterproofed by the dry cleaner.

Hand washing will work fine (and it's cheaper) for normal dirt. First remove the bag from the frame and remove any hold-open bars inside your pack. Next, wash the pack in warm water and mild soap

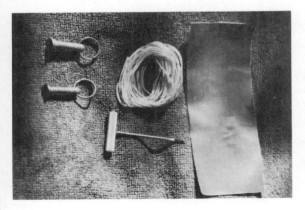

It's a good idea to carry an emergency pack repair kit on your extended hikes. Included should be two clevis pins, a roll of heavy thread, a sewing awl, and a piece of rip-stop tape.

either by hand or in a washing machine set on wash cycle. Presoak the bag if it's really dirty. After the bag has been washed, reattach it to the frame while the bag is still wet. Next set the frame and wet bag in a warm place with good ventilation; it should dry within an hour. After the pack has thoroughly dried, you may want to give it a coat of waterproofing (i.e., Scotchguard) . This treatment will help repel water and also help to resist staining in the future.

Store your pack in a dry place; an attic is ideal as long as the pack isn't in direct sunlight. Lacking an attic, you could store your pack in a closet or any other place that stays dry.

On the trail there are a few things that can go wrong with your pack, such as a rip in the material, a missing clevis pin, or a broken pack strap. I always carry a small repair kit to take care of such emergencies. My kit contains some heavy thread and rip-stop tape for repairing tears and broken straps and two extra clevis pins with split rings. I have never lost a clevis pin and don't know anyone else that has either, but I still carry the spares in case I get the chance to be the first.

Backpacking can be an exciting and rewarding experience. Equipment should be kept to a minimum and as simple as possible. The less you have to concern yourself with gear, the more you can enjoy the outdoors. So it makes sense to invest wisely. Your pack is your second most important piece of equipment. Choose both with care and then you can enjoy carefree hikes.

4

Sleeping Bags and Pads

by Clifford L. Jacobson

There is probably more mystique surrounding sleeping bags than any other item of equipment. Backpackers new to the sport are vaguely aware that a relationship exists between the quality of construction, weight, warmth of a bag, and cost. Exactly what this relationship is they're not sure, but to avoid any possibility of spending a night in the cold without suitable sleeping attire, many buy a bag that is too warm, too heavy, too bulky, and much too expensive. As a result, more tightly contoured, mummy-shaped winter bags are being sold to summer-season, sea-level trail walkers, than to high-altitude mountaineers for which they were originally intended. Backpacking with too much bag rather than too little is a spin-off from our affluent society and stems from clever advertising or from someone's single experience with a poor quality sleeping bag.

Many people rush out and buy the first bag they see, just because it is on sale, yet these same individuals wouldn't think of purchasing the first coat they find because it was a good deal. If you're in the market for a coat, you would probably choose a warm one for winter, a light one for summer, and perhaps something in between for the spring and fall months. Few hikers could afford to be so lavish when buying a sleeping bag. The important thing to realize, however, is that the one bag you do select must necessarily be a compromise, and thus it will be ideal for use throughout one, or at most, two seasons of the year.

A sleeping bag keeps you warm by trapping your body heat. The more dead air space there is within the bag's filler, the warmer the bag will be. The thickness of the insulator is the factor that determines the warmth of a sleeping bag—as long as the trapped air is not free to move. An air mattress, for example, contains a good deal of trapped air, but this air is constantly moving throughout each tube of the mattress as well as from one tube to another. As air molecules move, they lose heat to the ground and surrounding air, and as a result, sleeping on an air mattress in cold weather is somewhat akin to lying across the cooling coils of a refrigerator. If an air mattress were constructed with several baffles to slow down the movement of air within its tubes, it would be much warmer. And if the baffles were so closely spaced that no air could move at all, it would be incredibly warm. The reason foam sleeping pads insulate so well is because they trap air completely.

In addition to its primary function of stabilizing the movement of air, a sleeping bag filler must be resilient. Each morning you will tightly stuff your nicely fluffed bag into its small nylon carrying sack, and each evening you will draw it out and refluff the filler. After a period of many weeks or years, a poor quality insulator will lose sufficient resiliency so that it will not spring back to its original dimensions. In technical terms, the bag will lose its "loft" and because less loft means less trapped air, the sleeping bag will no longer be as warm.

Unfortunately, no sleeping bag fill is 100 percent resilient. In time, even the best materials—synthetic or natural—will lose some of their loft. Because the amount of loft your bag will lose over a given period of time depends upon how you treat it, suggestions for the care and cleaning of your sleeper are included in this chapter.

Waterfowl Down

The cottonlike insulation that lies just beneath the feathers of all birds is called down. A single fluff of down consists of a tiny central core from which hundreds of minute filaments branch out. When down from mature ducks and geese is used as a sleeping bag fill, thousands of its filaments entwine to produce a cellular network that effectively deadens the movement of air. The result is a warm and lightweight sleeping bag. For its weight, high-quality waterfowl down will trap more air than any other known material, and this includes the most modern of the polyesters. Being a natural fiber, the fluffy white (or gray) stuff is highly resilient, and a bag or garment filled with it can be stuffed into and pulled out of the smallest of spaces, thousands of times, with little loss of loft. Despite the recent development of excellent synthetics, down still remains the lightest, most thermally efficient, and compact (when stuffed) of all the sleeping bag fillers.

If ducks and geese were bred especially for the quality of their down, higher grades of this natural product would be more readily available. However, down is an agricultural byproduct. About 90 percent of the value of ducks and geese is in the eating; the rest is in the down. While it's generally agreed that large, mature waterfowl from cold climates produce the best down, it is also common knowledge that tough old birds aren't very palatable. So the trend is to the slaughtering of younger birds, for better taste, and this means it's getting harder and harder to find high-quality down.

Since you can't tell the quality of down inside a sleeping bag or garment by looking at it, you will have to trust the manufacturer. The only information you'll glean from the bag's label is the nature of the fill; in other words, goose down, duck down, or on Canadian bags, waterfowl down (a mixture of duck and goose down, or more probably, just duck down). The Federal Trade Commission does, however, require that all products labeled "down" possess at least 80 percent down. The remaining 20 percent allows for varying degrees of waterfowl feather fiber, nonwaterfowl feathers, and "miscellaneous" (which can mean anything). In short, even the best of the down-filled articles may be a long way from 100 percent down.

More reliable than the manufacturer's tag and FTC regulations is the filling or lofting power of the down. Unfortunately, there is no measuring device for loft that is universally accepted by all down merchants. So each processor determines for himself what is "good" down and what is bad. Some processors approach the problem more scientifically and use a simple graduated plastic tube and weighted piston to determine the loft. A standard test is to place 1 ounce of down into the plastic cylinder. The piston is then inserted in the cylinder and allowed to come to rest above the down column. The filling power of the down, in cubic inches per ounce, is read at the bottom of the piston. This method might be very accurate if all manufacturers and the Bureau of Standards agreed upon such matters as the diameter of the cylinder and the weight of the piston, but they don't. Each processor makes his own rules, and as a result, advertised loft readings vary widely. Nevertheless, advertised figures are still useful, for any manufacturer who advertises the lofting power of his down is at least proud of what he is selling and this means the customer is probably getting a decently made product. Those in the industry are in agreement that the general quality of down has deteriorated during the past few years. Today's high-quality downs seldom loft more than 600 cubic inches per ounce. A generation ago, 700 to 800 cubic-inch-per-ounce down was readily available.

Table I gives a rough idea of how much loft you need to sleep comfortably at the temperatures indicated. The values given are very approximate and depend upon your body metabolism, the closeness of the fit of your bag, when you last ate, and so on. For these reasons, reputable manufacturers don't like to state temperature ranges for their sleeping bags.

TABLE I

Approximate minimum temperature at which bag can be comfortably used in still air (Degrees Fahrenheit)	Loft* of filler in inches (one thickness of bag) required to attain desired minimum temperatures	
	Data supplied by U.S. Army Quartermaster	More realistic loft figures
40	1½	2
30	1¾	2½
20	2	3
10	2¼	3½
0	2½	4
−10	2¾	4½
−20	3	5

* It is important to realize that the advertised loft is a combined measurement of the top and bottom of the bag and thus must be halved for a realistic appraisal of the bag's minimum comfort range. Additionally, bag merchants tend to be overly optimistic in their measurements. The bag you buy probably won't loft as fully as that advertised.

A probably inaccurate rule of thumb is that 1 pound of goose down will increase the total loft of a snug-fitting bag by about 3 inches. This means that any bag that is filled with much more than 2 pounds of good down will be too warm for average spring and fall use, and intolerably hot in the summer. As mentioned, many backpackers are buying down bags that are much too warm for summer use.

Stabilizing the Down

A variety of different methods are used to stabilize down. These range from simply quilting the insulation into place, to the much warmer and necessarily more expensive method of overlapping the tubes to prevent cold spots. The most common baffle systems are illustrated below in the order of their thermal efficiency:

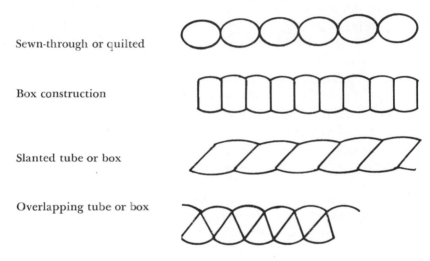

Sewn-through or quilted

Box construction

Slanted tube or box

Overlapping tube or box

Quilting is the most inexpensive and thermally inefficient way of building a down bag. With the down compressed to almost zero thickness at each seam, there are plenty of places for cold air to enter. Consequently, the few bags that are available in this style are primarily designed to be used as cold-weather liners for more conventionally constructed bags, or for use alone in very warm weather (above 50 degrees). Most quilted bags are very light—generally under 2½ pounds —and are extremely compact when stuffed. They are also easier to wash than more sophisticated bags because they don't have a delicate network of baffles.

Most of the better sleeping bags are of box or slant-box construction. Those with slanted baffles are warmer, more expensive and, because of the extra material used, slightly heavier than simpler box baffled models. A few high-quality, cold-weather bags are available in overlapping tube and double-quilt construction, but these tend to be heavy and very expensive. A simpler and less expensive solution for winter hiking is to use a quilted down liner inside your sleeping bag. Such a combination will be more versatile and just as warm as one of those "super bags."

Duck Down or Goose Down?

Keeping with the philosophy that the larger, older, and coldest climate-reared birds have the best down, we would have to say that goose down is best. But as pointed out earlier, the best quality goose down is not always available. Since there are no national standards for judging the quality of down, those clever adjectives like "genuine northern" down (northern California, perhaps?), "prime northern" down (picked at a prime time of the year?), and "high-loft" waterfowl down (how high is high?), which boldly adorn the bag's label, may be meaningless. If you are wise, you will pick your bag on the basis of quality of construction and not by what is written on the label. And this may be the best way to pick a bag, for it is doubtful that a manufacturer will pay close attention to quality sewing and detailing on a bag that is filled with inferior down or chicken feathers.

When purchasing a down bag, remember that you get exactly what you pay for. A cheap down bag is neither a good buy nor a good investment. Not only will such a bag be poorly sewn, but it may lack sufficient baffles to stabilize the down, and down that is not stabilized won't keep you warm.

The New Polyesters

With the exception of two new polyesters—Celanese Fortrel Polar-Guard, and duPont Polyester Fiberfill II—the synthetic fills are too heavy, too bulky, and not warm enough for use in a bag that will be carried on your back. Since their introduction in the early 1970s, the new polyesters have gained an almost cultlike following, and for good reason. First, Fiberfill II and PolarGuard are almost as efficient as down (it takes about 1.4 pounds of either of these synthetics to equal the thermal efficiency of 1 pound of down), and second, they are much less expensive. A modern polyester bag will weigh only 1 to 1½ pounds more than a comparable down model, and it will be only slightly less compact when stuffed into its nylon carrying sack. Moreover, both Fiberfill II and PolarGuard are highly resilient; both will spring back to their original dimensions even after repeated hard use and many washings. In fact, one manufacturer claims that if you wash its Polar-Guard sleeping bag properly, it will actually *increase* in loft, due to the mechanical separation of the polyester fibers.

But the greatest advantage of these new polyesters over down is the fact that they retain about 80 percent of their loft when soaking wet (as compared to almost nothing for down). Wet polyester also dries at least three times faster than the natural product. So for use around water, in rainy coastal areas, or for spending a night inside a snow cave, these new synthetics clearly have the edge.

Stabilizing Polyester

The new polyesters usually come in rolls of batting, and this batting must be cut and sandwiched between the shells of the sleeping bag. Since the batting is not loose, it doesn't need to be contained in tubes or baffled like down. It does, however, need to be sewn into place so it won't move around within the shell of the bag. The simplest method of stabilizing the filler is to quilt it into place. This, of course, produces cold spots, but it is the least expensive way to make a bag. A better method of securing the fill—one that eliminates surface seams—is to sew the edge of the batting directly to the edge of the bag's shell (called "edge stabilization"). The best polyester bags, though, use a variety of unique stabilization techniques. These range from double overlapping quilt construction to slanted, laminated affairs that supposedly allow the fill to loft to its maximum.

Foam-Filled Sleeping Bags

Not to be overlooked are some unique bags filled with polyurethane foam. Poly-foam is very light, nonallergenic, and incredibly warm. Like down, it dissipates body moisture very well, and, like polyester, it is extremely rugged. If a foam bag gets wet, you merely wring it out to restore the foam to its former thermal efficiency. Foam bags are less expensive than equally warm down models, but they are no cheaper than good polyester bags and are far less compact when stuffed (foam bags are usually rolled rather than stuffed). Additionally, they have a poor draping quality to them and so they tend to be drafty. Neverthe-

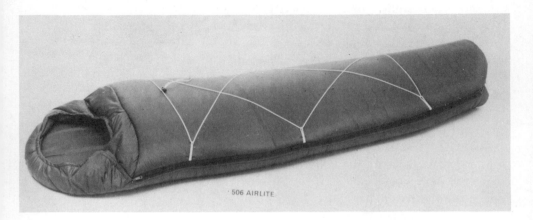

Besides down and synthetic-filled bags, a lightweight, polyurethane foam bag that stays warm even when wet is also available. Covered in nylon, it is 1¼ inches thick and needs no underpadding.

less, they are well liked by some hikers, and new developments in foam may eventually make them more attractive. In any case, they are worth looking into.

Down or Synthetic?

Much of the advertising emphasis behind synthetic sleeping bags centers around, "What do you do if you get your down bag wet?" The fact is, experienced backpackers almost never get their sleeping gear wet. If, for example, you use a ground cloth of some sort inside your tent (even though it has a sewn-in floor), you will eliminate many bouts with leaky floor seams. And if you line your bag's "waterproof" stuff sack with a plastic liner, you will never experience the displeasure of unstuffing a wet sleeping bag. Finally, the new nylon sleeping bag shells are very tightly woven, so even if you do get some water on your bag, it is doubtful that it will soak through and get the down wet. For expeditions and special conditions where wetness is a problem, bags filled with one of the new synthetics will be ideal. But for the average trailbound hiker, down still offers two very significant advantages over any other material—lighter weight and smaller stuffed size. Then, too, there's the luxurious feel of sleeping between down covers.

Shells

The shells of nearly all lightweight sleeping bags are made of either nylon taffeta or rip-stop nylon. Some manufacturers prefer taffeta over rip-stop, claiming that it is more abrasion proof and less likely to permit the down to escape. Other bag makers believe an equal weight of rip-stop is stronger and less likely to tear. While each material has its merits, the basic design of the bag and the care used in its construction is much more important.

Sleeping Bag Design

A confining, mummy-shaped bag will be warmer, lighter, and will stuff into a smaller sack than a similar rectangular bag of the same loft. For these reasons, experienced backpackers who pare every ounce select the smallest bag they can comfortably tolerate. In order to reduce cold spots in tight-fitting mummy bags, many manufacturers use what is called a differential cut. This means that the inner shell of the bag is cut smaller than the outer shell, much like the construction of a Thermos bottle. Differentially cut bags prevent extended knees and elbows from contacting the outer shell and reducing the thickness of the filler at these points.

A few manufacturers disagree with the differential cut theory. They claim this type of construction produces a bag that is rigid walled and drafty. Instead, they prefer to make both shells the same size (a space-filler cut). This construction produces a bag with many tiny folds and air pockets that surround the sleeper, thus eliminating drafts while adding insulation. However, space-filler cut bags—because of the additional material used—are heavier than similar differentially cut models, and their restrictive shells may not allow the down to loft to its fullest. These bags may also suffer from cold spots if you flail away at night with your knees and elbows. Because the differential versus space-filler cut argument has been simmering for the past few years, I won't add fuel to the fire by pretending to know which is best. My own bag is differentially cut, but when I bought it, I wasn't aware that there was any difference.

ARCTIC SLEEPER

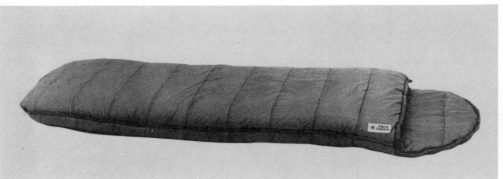

Top
A mummy-shaped bag, whether filled with prime goose down or one of the synthetic fills, is warmer, lighter, and will fit into a smaller stuff sack than a similar loft rectangular model.

Above
The rectangular bag does have its uses. Most can be unzipped completely and made into a comforter. If you've got two bags with complementary zippers, they can be put together to offer more warmth—and companionship.

Hood and Hood Closures

As explained in Chapter 2, your head is a very important part of
your anatomy—not just for thinking, but for conserving body heat.
So if you are really concerned about keeping warm, you should select
a sleeping bag with a hood. Hood closures range from good to bad,
and the good ones usually have attached to the drawstring a spring-
loaded toggle that locks the hood in a variety of positions. An easy-on,
easy-off hood closure will be especially appreciated on those cold, blus-
tery nights when nature calls. For winter use, when temperatures are
well below freezing, you would be wise to replace the plastic toggle with
a simple leather slider (most winter bags already come so equipped).
It's not that the plastic slider becomes brittle and breaks; it's the frigid
feel of the icy plastic against your skin that decides the issue.

A hooded bag is more expensive than one without. If you can't af-
ord the extra cost, you have the option of using a hoodless bag and
wearing a hat of some sort to bed.

Some hikers dispense with the hat routine and merely burrow down
into the bag, like a moth in a cocoon. Actually, this is an inefficient
way to keep warm; and if the temperature is very cold, such procedure
can be downright dangerous because the water vapor you exhale while
sleeping becomes trapped in the bag and lowers the efficiency of the
insulation. If sufficient moisture is expelled and the temperature is low
enough, the water vapor may condense and freeze, and you will, in
effect, be sleeping within a block of ice.

While a hat or hood will keep your head warm, it won't do much
for your nose. A knitted "nose cozy" is one solution. A loosely knitted
wool muffler or sweater placed over your face works just as well and
draws fewer snide remarks from friends. A muffler has the advantage
in that it can be wadded up above your shoulders to form a collar,
thus eliminating drafts.

All this discussion of hoods and hats is probably unnecessary if you
plan to hike at low altitudes in warm weather. The average summer
backpacker can get along very nicely with a hoodless bag.

A final suggestion, though. If you use a hoodless summer bag for
spring and fall hiking, sew a simple draft flap of soft wool or flannel
around the bag's opening. Make the flap about 9 inches wide and long
enough to go completely around the bag. Sew the top of the flap to the
bag and let the bottom hang free. This simple collar will eliminate
drafts and make the bag much more comfortable for sleeping.

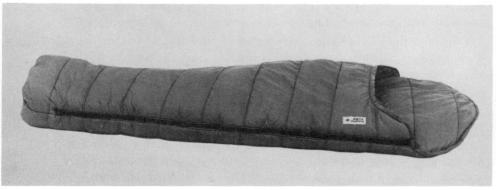

Top
For really cold-weather backpacking you can get an expedition-type bag. These usually have the highest amount of loft and come with a short center zipper. The less zipper in a bag, the less chance of drafts. Also, if the zipper breaks, you can still survive the night by pinning the bag together somehow.

Above
A full-zippered model, however, does afford you the opportunity for more comfort. If the confines become too hot, you can always open the zipper at the foot and give yourself some ventilation.

Zippers and Closures

A vast majority of good sleeping bags come equipped with full-length nylon zippers running down the right or left side (except for models with center zippers, you can ordinarily specify the side you prefer). A few bags, which are designed primarily for cold-weather use, have a short zipper (about 36 inches) that may be either side or center mounted. From the standpoint of insulation, the less zipper you

have the warmer the bag will be, for despite the best systems for eliminating zipper drafts, there's always some leakage. Also, if a short zipper
breaks, you may be able to clutch or pin the bag together and still survive the night. But if a full-length zipper breaks, you may be stuck
with a wide open sleeping bag, which, in frigid weather, can be serious
cause for concern. Nevertheless, most backpackers—even those on winter expeditions—will like full zippered models best since they are much
more comfortable throughout a wider range of temperatures.

Although manufacturers vehemently argue the advantages of side-
mounted zippers versus top-mounted ones, it's pretty much a matter of
personal choice, since it is doubtful that one method is really more
efficient than the other. The kind of zipper used, and how carefully it
is installed, is much more important. In short, good bags have the biggest, toughest zippers available. Cheap bags have small, lightweight
zippers that look attractive enough but cause nothing but problems.

Most good zippers have two-way sliders, allowing you to open the
foot of the bag for better ventilation on warm nights. If you unzip the
foot and leave your head uncovered, you can successfully use a warm,
mummy-shaped down bag (though with some discomfort) in very
warm weather. If you eliminate the foot opening though, the bag will
probably be unsuitable for use in temperatures much above 45 degrees.

While nearly all bags with compatible two-way zippers can be
joined, not all bags with one-way zippers can. Usually, if the zippers
can be fully separated at the foot, the bag will join with a similar
model. Though many mummy-shaped bags with full zippers can be
joined, the tapered, semirectangular models make a neater, more comfortable bed for two. So if you commonly share your bag with someone, you will probably prefer this style over the warmer, but more
confining, mummy shape.

Foot Shape

You can choose between a "flat foot" and a "box foot." Flat-footed
bags have a foot end similar to that of a folded-over quilt. For some
people, this type of bag is uncomfortable because the toes contact the
upper layer of fabric. A more comfortable—and more expensive—way
to build a sleeping bag is with a boxed foot. In this construction, an
oval or rounded piece of insulated material is inserted at the foot between the two layers of the bag. This raises the end of the bag 8 to 10
inches for more comfortable positioning of the feet. Those who are

delicate sleepers prefer this arrangement; those who aren't sleep "flat-footed," are just as comfortable, and save a few dollars.

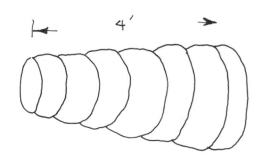

A mummy-shaped bag

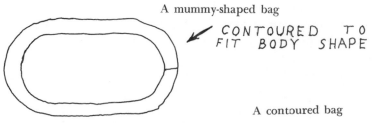

A contoured bag

On Buying a Sleeping Bag

Buying a sleeping bag is much like buying a car. In either case it's almost impossible to find one model that will do everything well. When selecting a car, you usually make your choice on the basis of the average use to which the vehicle will be put. You probably won't buy a pickup or a van if you plan to haul heavy items just once or twice a year, and you won't opt for four-wheel drive unless you have a real need for it. It makes good sense to choose a sleeping bag on a similar basis. If the majority of your trips will be taken in the summer, choose your bag accordingly. A lightweight bag will be easier to carry, more comfortable to sleep in, more compact when stuffed, and much less expensive than a more impressive winter model. For those once or twice a year winter trips, rent a warmer bag, or better yet, buy a quilted down liner for your summer bag. And don't neglect the value of your long johns and winter parka for cold-weather sleeping. In fact, the trend today is toward lightweight bags for winter use. To keep weight to a minimum, some devoted mountaineers use just a half bag, or "elephant's foot," as it is called. The elephant's foot is drawn up around their down or polyester parka and is tied around the waist with a cord.

Obviously, if you are planning an expedition, you will want the best bag possible, but even then, you can overspend. Whether a $150 bag is really better than a $100 model is debatable. You may wind up just paying for the name.

Once you have decided on the style bag you want (tapered rectangular, full-zip mummy, half-zip mummy, etc.), start writing for equipment store catalogs—all sorts of them. After you've compared bags from many manufacturers you should have a pretty good idea which model offers the most for the money. Before you buy, though, check local sources, especially in the early fall and after Christmas. Exceptional buys are sometimes possible during these sale times.

Finally, check the other items in a manufacturer's product line. A company that makes top-quality sleeping bags almost always makes excellent jackets, vests, and other outerware.

Junior-Size Sleeping Bags for Children

If you do a lot of backpacking with children and can find inexpensive junior-size sleeping bags, they may be worth buying, as their weight and stuffed size is considerably less than that of standard-size bags. However, youngsters grow out of these bags quickly, so ultimately you will need to purchase standard-size models for them. I have found it a mistake to buy an expensive down bag for a younger child. A single nighttime "accident" can make such a bag uninhabitable for the duration of the outing. Also, youngsters tend to treat sleeping bags (and other equipment) very harshly. A low-priced polyester bag is usually quite adequate for all but winter use.

Caring For and Cleaning Down-Filled Bags

After you've slept in your bag for a considerable number of nights it will begin to take on the aroma of a trail-weary hiking sock. Unless you sleep alone or can convince your tentmates that the odor has particular merit (perhaps in keeping pests away), you will be forced to clean your bag. A good many people are under the impression that washing a down bag destroys the down. This is not so. Studies by Recreational Equipment, Inc., have shown that proper washing with the right soap can actually increase the loft of the down. Such findings make sense because ducks and geese bathe regularly and would soon die if their down lost insulative value after each bath. But birds can replenish the oils in their down; sleeping bags can't. So everytime you clean or wash your bag, you will remove some of the natural oils. The problem then is to remove the unwanted oils—the dirty sweat that has seeped through the bag's shell into the down—without removing the essential oils.

When raw down is shipped to the processor it must be cleaned, and in the process of cleaning a considerable amount of the natural oils are removed (once you've seen and smelled raw down you wouldn't want it in its raw state). Proponents of "send the bag to the dry cleaners" capitalize on this fact by pointing out that dry-cleaning fluids are no more harsh than those used by the processor. The real issue, of course, is how much more oil can be removed from the down without affecting its performance. Most bag owners would agree that the answer is *None*!

Some years ago, down bag manufacturers commonly recommended hand washing as the safest way to clean their products. Evidently, "hand washing" has various connotations, for one person's successful method was another person's ruined bag. Because of numerous complaints, manufacturers took to recommending dry cleaning and adopted the attitude, "so what if you lose a little loft—at least you won't ruin the bag." To make sure you lose only a "little loft," you must find a cleaner that is familiar with down products, preferably one who uses the mild Stoddard cleaning fluid rather than the much more efficient perchloroethylene (or "perk" as it is called in the industry). Perk destroys down in quick order, while Stoddard fluid, being somewhat milder, takes considerably longer.

A better way to clean your bag is to hand wash it. Just lay the bag in your bathtub and cover it with lukewarm, soapy water. Use a very mild soap like Ivory Flakes, or one of the special down soaps like Fluffy, which is available from wilderness equipment mail-order houses. Let the bag soak for an hour or so, then use a sponge on the soiled shell. Be very gentle in handling the wet bag because it will be very heavy and if you are too rough the weight of the water may tear the delicate baffles loose.

Let the bag soak in the tub from 2 to 24 hours, depending on how dirty it is. Return occasionally to gently press the soapy water through the shell and into the down. *Warning*: Don't wring or twist the bag. You will ruin beyond repair both the shell and the down!

When the water in the tub has turned dark enough so that you are sure the bag is clean, begin the rinsing process. Rinse at least twice in tepid water and make sure you get *all* the soap out. Even the smallest amount of it will cause the down to mat. When the bag has been rinsed clean, pick it up—ever so gently so as not to harm the delicate baffles— and place it in your washing machine. Distribute the load evenly to balance the tumbler and set the machine on SPIN-DRY. *Don't use any other cycle!* For best results, spin-dry twice.

Next, remove the bag from the washer and take it to your local laundromat for drying. Don't use a standard-size home dryer for this operation because its smaller size may create hot spots that can scorch the bag. It is important that down sleeping bags be dried slowly, so locate a dryer with a low heat setting (most laundromats have at least one of these). Place the bag into the dryer along with a pair of canvas tennis shoes (laces removed). The shoes will flop around in the dryer and break up the down clumps, and this will make for faster and more uniform drying. Make sure the dryer really produces low heat. If it doesn't, run the dryer with the door ajar (you can jam a magazine or something over the door to keep the safety button depressed so it will run) and stop the machine every ten minutes or so to check the temperature. The laundromat will not replace your bag if you ruin it, even if their dryer is at fault. Drying will take about two hours—more if you have to fuss with the machine.

When thoroughly dry, take the bag home and hang it in the sun for a half-hour or so. This will remove the last bit of moisture and make it smell nice.

Some Do's and Don'ts For Down Sleeping Bags

1. *Do* wash your sleeping bag when it gets dirty—but not too often. Once a year is sufficient. To stretch the time between washings, sponge off the shell of the bag with a mild soap and warm water after each major use.

2. *Do* air your bag each day that you use it. Exposure to wind and sun will add to its life. Don't overdo it though; too much heat and ultraviolet light (several hours) can hurt the down.

3. *Do* use a waterproof stuff sack that is large enough for your bag. Stuffing bags into sacks that are too small is hard on the shell fabric, hard on the down, and still harder on your temperament.

4. *Do* unstuff your bag an hour or so before retiring and fluff air into it. This will allow ample time for the down to loft to its fullest.

5. *Do* use a ground cloth under your bag even if your tent has a floor. This will provide double protection in the event water gets into the tent through a leaky seam.

6. *Do* machine or sun dry your bag thoroughly before storing it for an extended period.

7. *Don't* dry clean your bag, even with a mild solvent, and never wash it with harsh detergents.

8. *Don't* roll a down sleeping bag. Instead, stuff it, a handful at a time, into its carrying sack. Rolling is harder on the down than stuffing is.

9. *Don't* yank your bag out of its stuff sack. Pull it gently! This will save wear and tear on both baffles and stitching.

10. *Don't* leave your bag in a waterproof stuff sack for long periods of time. A few days won't hurt anything, but several weeks might. At home, store the bag flat on a bed, over a hanger, or in an oversized, breathable cotton or burlap sack.

11. *Don't* ever use high heat to dry a wet bag. The heat can burn the oils out of the down and destroy the nylon shell.

12. *Don't* lend your bag out. Even your best buddy may not know how to treat it.

Caring For and Cleaning Synthetic-Filled Sleeping Bags

Many of the rules given for down bags don't apply to synthetic bags because synthetics are much tougher than down. For example, you can machine wash or dry clean polyester bags with no harmful effects. Also, sustained exposure to sunlight doesn't hurt them. Common sense, of course, dictates that these bags should be dried slowly and should never be stored wet.

The "do's and don'ts" given for the care of down bags are nevertheless good guidelines for what and what not to do with the synthetics. Machine washing, for example, is necessarily more harmful than hand washing, and while the batting in these bags may not be hurt by the washing machine, the sewing might. Machine-washed bags fall apart much faster than those washed by the more time-consuming hand method. Stuffing a bag rather than rolling it seems less hard on both filler and shell, and a stuff sack that is too small will be hard on both the filler and its stitching.

In conclusion, if you treat your synthetic bag like a good down model, you will likely get a lifetime of service from it. But if you store it wet, track mud on it, and treat it in other abusive ways, its advantages over the natural product will be negligible and you will find yourself investing in a new bag after only a few outings.

Sleeping Pads and Air Mattresses

One of the main virtues of the modern backpacking bag—be it down or polyester—is its ability to be stuffed into a small space. This compressibility, while a virtue when the bag is confined within its carrying sack, is a disadvantage when bedtime rolls around. This is because the weight of your body compresses the filler beneath to almost zero, thus reducing the warmth. This is less of a problem with bulkier synthetic bags than with down ones, but it still exists. The standard solution is to use a pad or mattress of some sort beneath the bag. Many backpackers prefer one of the closed-cell foam pads like Ensolite, Thermobar, or Volarfoam. Each cell of these pads is sealed, so it is completely watertight and can thus be used as a life preserver or buoyancy aid for an unexpected stream crossing.

Closed-cell pads range in thickness from about 1/4 inch to 1/2 inch, and in length from about 36 inches to 72 inches. Obviously, the thicker and longer pads are warmer and more comfortable to sleep on, but they are also heavier and bulkier. Generally speaking, a 1/4- or 3/8-inch-thick pad, long enough to reach from the neck to midthigh (about 48 inches), is adequate except for use on snow. Sufficient clothing can usually be piled under your unprotected lower legs and feet to make up for the short length of the pad.

Comfort-wise, open-cell urethane foam pads are a step up from closed-cell pads. But because the open-cell foam is three to four times more compressible than the closed-cell variety, a considerably greater thickness of it is required to obtain equal thermal efficiency. Also, unless these pads are protected with a waterproof outer covering, they will soak up water like sponges if they get wet.

Urethane foam pads are usually about 1 1/2 inches thick and are available with either waterproof or nonwaterproof covers. A major advantage of the nonwaterproof cover is that it allows the pad to absorb the body moisture that would ordinarily remain trapped in the bottom of your sleeping bag. Nonbreathable pads—open or closed cell—won't take in perspiration, and thus become impossibly hot in warm weather.

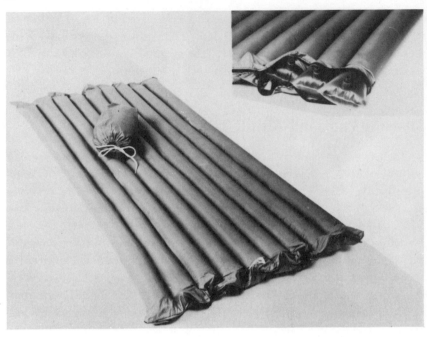

Inflatable mattresses are the most comfortable underpadding you can get. This modular model inflates in about 75 seconds (breath-power) and comes with nine air chambers and a separate spare tube. Deflated, it rolls to a bundle of 3½×7 inches.

For this reason, many experienced backpackers prefer breathable urethane foam in the summer, and Ensolite, Thermobar, or Volarfoam in the winter.

Air mattresses, which were passé a few years ago, seem to be making a comeback. In all probability, the switch by many backpackers from down to synthetic bags has had much to do with it. For comfort, an air mattress can't be beat, but even a good air mattress can develop leaks, and good or bad, it must be inflated by lung power each night (unless, of course, you carry a bulky foot-operated air pump). The best lightweight air mattresses are heavier, more compact when folded, and more expensive than three-quarter length closed- or open-cell foam pads. Their major drawback, however, is their lack of insulation, which makes them unsuitable for use with a down bag in cool or cold weather. This problem can be solved by placing a 36-inch length of ¼-inch-thick Ensolite on top of the mattress. The Ensolite, which

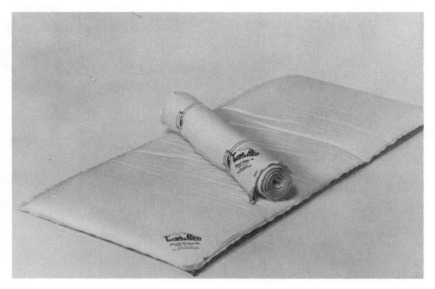

The "ThermaRest" pad combines the insulative qualities of foam with the comfort of air. Essentially, it's an open cell pad with a sealed cover and an inflation valve. To inflate you open the valve and roll out the pad. Once it's fully opened out, close the valve and it's ready.

weighs but a few ounces, provides the warmth; the air mattress provides the comfort. But then you wind up carrying two pads.

An unusual new mattress that has recently appeared on the market is a self-inflating foam pad called the "ThermaRest." The ThermaRest combines the virtues of both air mattress and foam pad into a single lightweight unit. Essentially, the mattress is an open-cell foam pad with a sealed waterproof cover and an inflation valve. To inflate the pad from its rolled position, you merely open the valve. The compressed open-cell foam absorbs the air and within a few minutes, the pad expands to its normal thickness. When the air pad is fully inflated, you close the valve to lock the air in.

In use, the ThermaRest gives almost as much support as an air mattress, but because of its foam interior it provides valuable insulation. To deflate the pad, you merely open the valve and force out the air by rolling up the pad. When the air is expelled, you seal the valve, and the pad, which resembles a large, wrinkled prune, is now ready for packing.

After using one of these pads for the past two seasons, I'm completely sold on it. My only reservation is its cost—about $30 which puts it beyond the reach of many backpackers.

Now that I've taken the mystique out of sleeping bags and pads, you'll be able to match your gear with your habits and budget. Maybe you'll even start sleeping better on the trail. And all the while you thought it was insomnia.

5

Tents

by Louis V. Bignami

If you're the type of backpacker who cuts half the handle off your toothbrush to save weight, you're probably not going to use a tent for most summer trips. However, a tent does have a secure place in the backpacking world. It provides a control of your sleeping environment that you can get in no other way; it will keep you dry when conditions change for the worse; it will keep bugs and other creepy-crawlies off you and your gear; it will protect you from the wind; and, if nothing else, it will give you a private place to change clothes in increasingly crowded backcountry camps. But most importantly, if you're trapped by an early or late-season snowstorm, a tent can even save your life.

Years ago tent selection wasn't much of a problem because the army pup tent was just about the only design available. Today, however, there must be more than 100 designs, most of them good, that you can choose from. So to reduce this to some kind of order we'll deal with design types by category before getting down to actual design and construction points that determine a good buy in this confusing field.

Tent and Shelter Classifications

1. Tarps, ponchos, and single-sheet shelters
2. Tube tents—plain and fancy

3. I-pole tents
4. A-frame tents
5. Winter expeditionary tents
6. Three- and four-man tents
   a. Large A-frames
   b. Tepee designs
   c. Geodesic domes and pop tents

Each of these tent designs best serves one or more functions. Whatever your choice, it should provide the maximum of flexibility with the minimum of weight. Cost should only be a minor factor, for quality lightweight tents can't be cheap and durable too.

Tarps, Ponchos, and Single-Sheet Shelters

If you're camping mostly in the summer in areas where rain is usually just a quick thunderstorm, then one of these designs may do the job, particularly if you have a combination groundcloth cover for your bag.

Most tarps can be pitched like a pup tent, and you can use the rainfly from a conventional tent as a tarp when you don't want to carry the entire tent. If you're walking in an area where bugs aren't a problem, this type of arrangement will be sufficient in most conditions. It won't work if there's a heavy storm or strong winds, and bugs can drive you crazy in the early spring, but tarps are a minimum solution, especially in combination with a poncho that you can use to cover your sleeping bag. Most tarps and rainflys are nylon and should have reinforced tags or grommets for the support lines, usually simple nylon cord. You can use a short pole or two from your tent, or two regular poles to keep your fly or tarp pitched in wet weather.

Perhaps a cheaper solution is a plastic sheet with Visklamp fastenings. Make sure you get a sheeting at last .004 inch thick. An 8×9-foot piece will weigh about a pound and shouldn't cost more than a couple of dollars. Since this sheeting has no grommets you have to use Visklamps—clever wire and rubber ball fasteners that weigh about an ounce—to fasten it. Four or six Visklamps will give you enough flexibility in pitching to get along, and you'll need an equal number of pieces of short nylon line and four pin stakes for ground connections. This system will work in moderate conditions, but in heavy winds watch out! If the flapping doesn't drive you to distraction, the eventual

The Pioneer by Gerry is actually a versatile tarp that can be pitched in one-, two-, or three-man configurations. It measures 8 feet, 10 inches in length and 8 feet, 6 inches in width. It's made from 2.5-ounce rip-stop nylon, coated for water repellency.

tearing of the sheet will. Still this is cheap and will stand up for a couple of trips before it wears out, making it a good summer solution while you're deciding what kind of "tent" you'd like to buy.

Tube Tents

Tube tents are really a modification of the plastic sheet and are shaped, like the name says, in a tube. They have the advantage of quick pitching. All you need to do is run a line between two trees or rocks, string the tent on the line, and throw yourself and your gear inside. You can use rocks or gear to spread the bottom of the tube so your tent assumes the proper A-shape.

Instead of a tube tent or tarp you can usually get along in reliable weather with just a poncho, but this is a solution that won't do on trips

Another example of a single-sheet shelter is the Frostline tarp tent. This one is made from a kit, meaning you have to sew it together yourself. This type of tent will keep you reasonably dry in drizzles, but strong winds, heavy storms, and bugs will cause problems.

The Tunnel Tent, made by Lowa, has plenty of sit-up room inside, measures nearly 9 feet in length, and has two T-shaped doors at the ends. It can be pitched with only one anchor at each end and is sturdier than a tarp tent because of the low profile and internal support system.

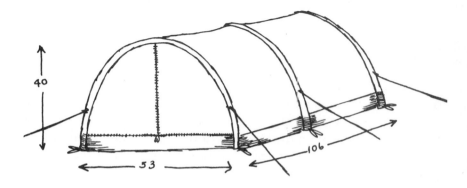

longer than a couple of days. I feel very strongly that you can—and should—take a tent along, especially now when freeze-dried foods and ultralight gear have made packs so light.

I-Pole Tents

This is the traditional army pup tent design and probably the most common type in use today. Its advantages are clear: easy erecting, reasonable internal area for the amount of fabric, simple design, and cheap construction. The disadvantages are equally clear: you have to crawl around the center pole in the entrance, the tent is not self-supporting, you usually have external guys to trip over—the front guy is a particular hazard here—and you could have a sagging problem in models without catenary cutting of the fabric. In cheaper models you'll also have a condensation problem because they don't come with a rainfly. Still these are a refined design within design limits and such a tent from a quality mountaineering house can serve you reasonably well.

A special-purpose modification of this type of tent is the netting bug tent that several manufacturers make. In these tents the entire roof and door is mosquito netting, though most come with a rainfly to pitch over the top. No other tent is as comfortable in hot, muggy weather or when desert camping. It's a very useful option that most backpackers aren't aware of in areas where bugs and very hot weather are found in combination. Gerry makes the best one of these I've used, but you can check around for other brands. Be particularly sure of the way the netting is sewn in and how the pitched stresses are distributed because the light netting won't provide support, just bug protection.

A-Frame Tents

If you were to survey skilled backpackers, you'd probably find that more than two-thirds are now using A-frame tents. Still reasonably light, these designs incorporate such features as a separate rainfly, shock-corded poles that fit into pockets in the front and rear of the tent so you have an unobstructed entrance, and self-supporting design. Some use tabs on the sides of the tent to increase internal capacity. This is often the only spot where these tents incorporate outside lines that you might trip over.

An example of the I-Pole tent is the Gerry Mosquito. It has one pole construction and measures 7×4.5 feet. Perhaps the brightest feature of this particular model is that the canopy material is nylon mesh to keep air circulating and bugs out. Of course, it can only be used in milder temperatures.

This design is priced between simple I-pole tents and the most complicated winter expeditionary tents. The A-frame is probably the most flexible and most useful one in the $100 to $200 range. The only disadvantage of this design is size. I'm over 6 feet and 200 pounds and I find that those sizes with floors smaller than 7½×5 feet just won't hold two adults and their gear. However, this size, or smaller, will do in a pinch and is especially suited to summer camping where the weather is somewhat uncertain.

Tents of this type from North Face, Sierra Designs, Gerry, REI, EMS, Browning, and the Ski Hut are all recommended, and you can buy kits to make your own tent at about a 40 percent savings from Frostline and Holubar. But be sure to check out other manufacturers and kit makers. You'll probably be able to come up with a bargain.

The Crestline Expedition from Recreational Equipment, Inc., is a double A-frame designed for year-round use. It has a vestibule and tunnel entrance at one end for storing gear and cooking.

Winter Expeditionary Tents

These are the Rolls-Royces of the tenting field and provide the maximum amount of portable shelter. Most use double A-frame support systems and feature snow flaps, enclosed vestibules for gear storage and cooking, cook holes in the floor, and frost liners. Exceptionally stable and entirely self-supporting in normal conditions but with the capacity to have tie lines used in super bad weather, these tents are really a specialty item for those who climb high or do a lot of ski mountaineering. None of these tents are cheap, most are fairly heavy for their size, and you shouldn't even consider one unless you have a clear and frequent use. If you're only going to snow camp once or twice a year, you'd be better off renting one, and using a lighter, cheaper tent for general use.

Three- and Four-Man Tents

Tents larger than the traditional two-man come in all sorts of sizes, shapes, and weights. You can get I-pole, A-frame, and winter expeditionary tents in larger sizes. If you do a lot of car camping and only backpack on short weekend trips, you'll probably find tents in this size range are worth the extra price and weight. This is particularly true if you backpack early and late in the year, or in locations where you can be tent-bound for several days. The added space is well worth it.

In this larger size you'll also find a great number of shapes. Geodesic domes, modified tepees, and pop tents are the most common types, and each has special advantages and problems.

Geodesic dome tents are the portable examples of Buckminster Ful-

More and more manufacturers are starting to make specialty tents that defy categorizing. The Pleasure Dome from Sierra Designs is a three-man tent that features two vents near the peak, two zippered and screened windows, and a large zippered screen door. The retail prices of these specialty tents are around $200.

PLEASURE DOME

One of the most unusual configurations around is the North Face Oval In-Tention. It's a geodesic dome that utilizes six shock-corded wands (two each of three different lengths) and a shape-defining skin. It can be pitched in about six minutes. Most of the interior space is usable and because of the external wand suspension the tent is entirely self-supporting. It sells for around $285.

ler's design and they offer the most interior space for surface size. While there are several designs in the field, the only one I've extensively tested is North Face's Oval InTention. I consider this the best wet-weather tent I've ever used. Its design has several major advantages. First, almost all the interior space is usable and the tent lives bigger than it looks because you don't have the wasted space you find in the sides of A-shapes. Second, the external wand suspension system makes the tent entirely self-supporting. Since there are no long distances between support points, it barely flaps in the strongest winds. Third, the rainfly attaches quickly since the locking points are at the base of the wand supports, making it easy to find them in the dark. About the only drawbacks of this tent are a condensation problem on the lower sides in mild weather and the fact that the entrance is on the long axis. But overall, it's a super tent for wet weather.

Modified tepee designs are also common in this size range and these offer the advantage of standing room under the center support. North Face's Morning Glory and Dandelion are two examples of this type of design, but there are several other good models. All these tents are usually the top-of-the-line model of any manufacturer, and you can be sure that they are of the finest possible workmanship. I find it a good idea to subtract one person from the recommended capacity if the weather is going to be rough. Still, for a family, three- and four-man tents will serve well. Most run $200 or more, and about 10 pounds, but this includes the weight of rainflys, poles, and stakes. That may put them slightly over the weight capacity for the average backpacker, but the choice is yours.

Pop tents are also becoming more and more common in areas where distances are short. Most are a little heavy for their size, thus making them best suited for weekend use. However, like most other areas in design and function, this is a matter of taste, and these tents sure are easy to put up.

Remember, though, whichever design you choose, you should never buy a model "cold." If possible, spend a few weekends in rented or borrowed tents so you'll have the chance to make actual field comparisons. Any tent from a quality, specialty manufacturer should last you ten years or more. You'll be well repaid for your initial testing efforts with many years of use. If you can't test, then you can still make some determinations as to quality by checking the materials and construction features of a prospective tent. Designers' ideas may vary some here, but the signs of quality are plain.

Your first option should be tent material. Cotton was used up to World War II, but it has since been replaced by nylon. The latter is twice as strong, much more durable, and not susceptible to mildew and other water damage. But there are several types of nylon netting, rip-stop materials, and nylon taffeta, and each one has its own special application.

The floor of your tent, and normally the first 6 to 12 inches of the sides, should be waterproof nylon in order to prevent ground moisture from seeping into your tent. This means that the only parts of the tent not waterproofed are those parts not covered by the rainfly. Nylon taffeta, with its higher resistance to abrasion, is used in the floor after it has been coated with a polyurethane or polymeric coating.

The main parts of the tent will normally be rip-stop nylon. This type of fabric breathes, so you don't get condensation inside your tent, and the intermittent heavier fibers in the material help keep holes from tearing or spreading. Hence, the name.

Since the tent's top is untreated nylon, you'll need a rainfly that pitches over the tent in wet weather. This fly is usually treated with the same waterproofing material as the tent's bottom. In addition to keeping rain off your tent, this surface also acts as a condensation trap on its underside. In hot weather you'll also find that tents pitched with rainflys are much cooler than those without. Note that almost all quality tents include rainflys as part of the original package. However, if you don't have a fly, you can always rig one from a plastic tarp.

Whichever option you choose you should check to see that the rainfly has its own system of ties and supports and that it is suspended above the tent and touches the tent only at the poles or support wands. If your rainfly bags down in the middle and touches the tent's inner fabric, it will cause condensation and, eventually, a leak.

With this combination of fabrics your tent should remain dry under almost any conditions. You might find that you still can have some condensation between the Ensolite pad under your sleeping bag and the tent's bottom. This is not leakage and should be expected.

All good tents are equipped with a fully netted entrance and a vent system. Nylon mesh is the standard here, and you should compare models for mesh size. My own feeling is that you can never get a mesh too tight for no-see-ums and snow mosquitoes.

Vents along the sides of the tent, plus either vented tubes, windows, or panels at the back of the tent, will give you the control you need over air circulation for comfort in varying conditions. All should be netted and have zippered covers you can close in very cold weather.

These zippers, and the zippers of your tent's entrance panel and mesh netting, are very important to your tent's wear. Since they are the only really movable parts of your tent, they tend to be the first things to wear out. Metal used to be the standard here, but more and more companies are finding that nylon zippers are stronger and won't freeze in cold weather. Entrance zippers on the netting and rip-stop panels should be designed so that they have a pull at each end. This makes getting in and out easier and lets you adjust the amount of air coming in the front of your tent.

Note that you should never leave a tent open during the day. I always keep the entrance netting panel zipped shut to keep bugs out. In hot weather you'll find all the bugs in the area using your tent as a sun shade and they'll be there to greet you unless you close the tent up tight.

The pole or wand system that your tent uses for support is a major part of its durability factor. Good poles are made of light, aircraft alloy aluminum and should be shock-corded so the pieces stay together and are easy to assemble. If you've ever ended up on site with half a pole, you already know how much of an advantage this is.

Stakes for your tent are usually plastic pegs or aluminum pins that are bent into a "U" shape. Each type has its advantages and I've found that I have a set of each for all my tents and pick the type to take depending on the ground I expect to find. The pegs can be driven into hard ground with a boot or rock, but the pins are lighter and sharper and I usually take them. With a self-supporting tent like the Oval In-Tention, you may find you don't really need stakes at all. Unless it gets really windy the weight of your gear will be enough to keep your tent in one place.

Even assuming that you check all the materials in your tent, you may still find that it isn't properly put together. An infallible clue to quality of construction is the lack of raw edges on the seams. All seams should be bound or flat felled, and all stresses should be reinforced. Check, too, to see how the pole holders are reinforced. Most tents use a second layer of heavier fabric here, which is a vital precaution against early signs of wear. While you're checking for this you should check on the type of thread used. Nylon thread is fine because it won't cut through the nylon fabric like some kinds of polyspun or Dacron thread. But the Dacron thread, covered with cotton, is also a good solution since the cotton expands when wet to fill thread holes in the fabric and thus reduce seam leakage.

If you check these features and pick a tent from one of the many specialty manufacturers, you won't go wrong. All you have to do is take care of the tent properly and it should last ten years or more.

Proper tent care has always seemed to me to be more a matter of personality than procedure. Some people are just more careful with their equipment than others. But even if you're in the careless group, like I am, you can double your tent's life by recognizing the problem areas.

The first thing you have to do is keep your tent clean inside and out.

My rule is "no boots in the tent." Boots pick up dirt, branches, and rocks that are designed to cut your tent's floor. Besides, taking off your boots in camp and putting on a pair of down booties is a super feeling. Another method that works for me is to use a 2-foot square of heavy plastic for a step-in spot inside the tent, or when its wet, just outside the tent so you can squat and swing your bottom inside. Then remove your boots and get inside. This square also serves as a handy drying platform inside your tent for wet boots and gear.

Damage to the bottom of your tent can also come from rocks and small pine cones under your pitch. When I'm car camping or spending my first night at the trailhead, I use a piece of very heavy plastic as a ground cloth under the tent. If you drive up to the trailhead the night before a weekend trip and pitch in the dark like I do, you'll find this will save you lots of wear. Another good idea where weight isn't a problem is to use a piece of canvas as an inside liner.

During your stopover days on the trail you should take the time to clean your tent. Self-supporting types can be picked up and shaken so all loose dirt will come forward. Other types of tents should be brushed out. A damp pair of Ragg socks makes an excellent broom for this.

In use a good tent will hold up exceptionally well if you care for it. As part of this care, don't use propane lamps or stoves inside without first putting them on a heavy piece of canvas. All you have to do is tip a lantern or stove over and the hot parts will burn through *any* fabric. Incidentally, the only tents that really represent a fire hazard are the cotton ones that are treated with flammable water-repellent chemicals. You'll have to search pretty far to find one of these now because almost all tents on the market today meet flammability standards set by the government. Consider yourself lucky if you *can't* find a cotton tent.

When I come back from a trip my first step is to pitch my tent in the backyard and hose it down. Then I take a good look at the inside for food stains—Hershey bars or gorp in bed can produce these—and if necessary I use warm water and a mild soap solution to remove the stains. The outside of the tent is checked next. Rainflys collect sap from trees, plus the offerings of birds, so they should be hosed and sponged. Then I check the outside bottom of the tent for mud. After the whole tent is dry I take it down, and check all nylon lines for fraying. If any are frayed, I'll heat seal them with a match.

Now I'll turn the tent over and check the bottom. I find that a little touch up of abraded areas with seam sealant will prevent holes from happening. If you do get a puncture you can fix it in the field with

tape and then sew on a patch at home. Now I am ready to return the
tent to the stuff sack. It's important to be careful here. The best way to
put holes in a tent is to jam it in along with wire tent pins. No matter
how careful you are to put the pins in their own section of the sack,
they always seem to escape. My solution is to place the pins in their
own sack separate from the tent. I just tie the pull cords of both stuff
sacks together so I don't forget the pins on my next trip.

Pitching a tent in the field shouldn't be a problem if you stop early
enough in the day so you still have light. If you're going to camp in a
wooded area, check the ground for cones and sap. Some types of trees
shed more of these than others, and some of our dropping giant western pine cones can put a big hole in a rainfly. Pitching under a dead
tree can be fatal—so don't. Dead trees tend to blow over and can also
attract lightning. My own favorite pitches are usually among rocks on
the lee sides of a ridge or near a stream. Don't, however, pitch on
meadows or right on the edge of a stream. Meadows are damp and
streams produce insects that can be a problem. If you're 20 feet or so
higher than the water, this can be avoided. But if you get too far from
water you'll spend all your time making trips to the creek, unless you
carry a very large water bag.

When you're pitching check to be sure you're on a slight rise so water will run away from rather than into your tent. One of the funniest
things I ever saw was two buddies in Oregon who, against everyone's
advice, pitched in a "nice little gully out of the wind." The wind
brought a storm, the gully became a brook, and they had to wade out
carrying wet bags. Fortunately, we were right at the trailhead and had
lots of extra gear so this incident was funny. But in desert areas susceptible to flash floods, it could be fatal.

The actual process of pitching a tent is pretty simple if you've prac-
ticed it at home first. You just check the spot for debris, square up the
tent, peg it down reasonably tight, keep the tension on guy lines, and
up it goes. If you're with a friend, one of you should get inside without boots, and the other can hand the gear in. Then, while the inside
man lays out pads and fluffs bags, the outside man can go for water
and get a stove or fire started.

Getting your tent up should always be your first step after you've
arrived at your overnight area and checked about for the best site.
Then you can run off and trout fish or whatever and your camp will
be ready for you when you return. This simple step will keep you from
having to set up in the dark or in the rain.

Selecting and using a tent well is really a matter of common sense, but you have to be aware of potential problems and take a little care if you're going to get maximum use for your money. I've had a Ski Hut tent since 1955 and it's still serving my needs reasonably well. There have been remarkable design and construction advances since that time. So, with a little care there's no doubt that present-day tents can last you as long or longer.

6

Food and Cooking Gear

by Don Geary

Besides all of the other things that backpacking does for you, it builds one heck of an appetite. And what could be more rewarding, after hours of walking through forest and meadow, than a dinner of lasagna or shrimp creole? It wasn't very long ago that about the only thing a hiker had to look forward to, food wise, was a simple meal of bacon and beans, but in recent years food for hikers has undergone some changes—both good and bad. The results are a vast selection to choose from and a weight loss that is astounding.

The length of your trek determines, of course, what type of food you should carry. For example, on a day hike you can usually stuff a sandwich and a few candy bars into your pockets and not have to worry about any real meals. On weekend hikes you still have quite a bit of leeway as to the type of food that you take along. Weight just isn't that important if you're going to be out for only one night, but if you plan to stay on the trail for longer periods, say three days, then you should give some serious consideration to what you carry.

In warm weather, you can expect to burn up approximately 3,000 calories per day of walking. In cold weather, caloric needs run about 4,000 to 4,500 calories per day. Obviously, if you want to keep on walking, you have to stoke your internal furnace with enough calories to keep your body running efficiently.

Before you can plan to replenish calories to your system you must know which foods contain the most calories per unit of weight. Briefly, calories come from three principal sources in foods: fats, protein, and carbohydrates. Fats generally have about twice as many calories as proteins or carbohydrates and, therefore, would seem to be the most efficient food. But since fats take longer to digest, they release calories into your system over a longer period of time. Carbohydrates, on the other hand, release calories almost immediately. Therefore, in order to replenish calories while on the trail, you should eat more fats at the last meal of the day and let them serve as a reservoir of calories. During the day eat foods that are high in carbohydrates for quick energy and immediate caloric needs.

Good sources of carbohydrates are sugars, starches, and celluloses. Fats are present in meats, cooking oils, and butter or margarine. Protein can be found in meats, nuts, and milk. Many foods contain combinations of fat, protein, and carbohydrates so really precise, balanced meal planning is difficult. But as long as you know generally where calories come from, you can use this information as a rule of thumb.

Several of the makers of freeze-dried and other foods for hikers now specify the number of calories and the grams of fats, protein, and carbohydrates contained in their food. You may find this information useful when planning your trip. Every pound of excess body fat contains about 3,500 calories. If you don't increase your caloric intake when you're out hiking or are engaged in other physical activity, naturally your body will obtain the extra calories it needs from the excess baggage you are carrying around, namely fat. And after a few weeks on the trail that excess fat should start dropping off. In any event, you can be certain that you will burn up considerably more calories while hiking than at home or at the office.

By this time you may have realized that there has been no mention of vitamins or minerals. You shouldn't be overly concerned with them because you probably have enough in your system to last for at least a month. Trying to plan vitamin-packed meals for the trail only makes the planning more complex than it has to be. Don't worry about vitamins but do try to cover your caloric needs.

Food for Hikers

As mentioned earlier, if you're only planning an overnight trip there's no real need to concern yourself with lightweight foods. But if your trip will last three days or longer you had better be concerned with the food you pack or your back will be the first to let you know that you could have planned better.

Basically there are two types of drying processes that make food lighter: hot-air drying (dehydration) and freeze-drying. Dehydration is not a new preservation method, having been around in various forms for centuries. The smoking of meats and fish is a form of dehydration. For our purposes, dehydration means food that has been processed using a combination of hot air and high temperatures.

Spray drying is a method of dehydration used to remove the moisture from such liquids as fruit juices and milk. The fluids are squirted through nozzles and dry air is passed through the spray to carry off the moisture. The resultant crystals are what you get when you buy powdered milk or fruit juice mixes.

Tunnel drying is another hot-air dehydration method commonly used for many types of meat and vegetables. In this process the food is laid out on wire racks or continuously moving belts that pass through a long tunnel. Inside the tunnel hot air is blown over the food and the moisture is thereby removed.

Most dehydration methods remove approximately 95 percent of the moisture from the food. Such foods store well. Before using dehydrated foods you must add water (usually hot) and wait for the food to *re-*hydrate. Unfortunately, dehydrated foods look a bit strange to the uninitiated. The hot-air treatment causes the food to shrivel and lose much of the original color. As an example of dehydration, compare a raisin with a fresh grape. They're not very similar in appearance, but they both taste good.

Freeze-drying, technically known as vacuum sublimation, is a relatively new process for removing the moisture from foods and is often referred to as the greatest breakthrough in food preservation since the tin can. Freeze-dried coffee is one common example. In this process the food is quickly frozen at minus 40° to 50°F. in a chamber where conditions approach near vacuum—approximately 1/1000 of an atmosphere. As a result of the low pressure and temperature the water in the food passes directly from ice crystals to vapor without ever becoming liquid. Thus, the cell structure of the food remains intact. In other words, a piece of apple looks the same as it did before the process, not shriveled grotesquely as with dehydrated foods. Approximately 97 percent of the moisture is removed from the food during the freeze-drying process but all of the nutrients and vitamins remain in.

As you may have guessed, freeze-drying is the most expensive method of removing moisture from foods. This is probably due to the fact that freeze-drying is done in relatively small batches that require more handling and attention than other methods of drying. High processing costs inevitably lead to high selling prices, but this doesn't seem to deter serious hikers in search of tasty, lightweight food.

Taste, "fillingness," and visual appeal are governed more by personal idiosyncrasies than anything else. Taste, in most freeze-dried foods, is pretty close to the real article. Obviously, a vegetable fresh from the garden will have a taste that can't be equaled in a vegetable that has been processed by any method. But freeze-dried meats and vegetables come about as close to the fresh food as possible, and are usually far better tasting than dehydrated foods.

Fillingness of meals depends on such factors as your personal metabolism rate, how hard you have walked, the size of your stomach, and how hungry you are when the meal is served. Most freeze-dried foods will be in packages marked "Serves Two" or "Serves Four" and this can be an aid when shopping for meals. However, many people have found that two people often have no problem eating a meal designed and labeled for four. In fact, I have seen children devour a two-person meal and ask for more. As a rule, you should carry meals designed for more than are in your group or, knowing that the meals will be a little on the scant side, plan to supplement them with other foods.

Visually, freeze-dried foods win hands down in any comparison with dehydrated foods. As mentioned above, the cell structure of the food is not altered and thus the appearance of the food remains much the same as before processing.

You can buy freeze-dried meals from your local equipment dealer or directly from one of the several companies that produce these foods. A list of companies that sell freeze-dried meals (and over 175 main dish meals are available) is at the end of this chapter. Most large supermarkets also sell a wide selection of freeze-dried foods. Some obvious examples are freeze-dried coffee, soup mixes, and fruit drink crystals. Other lightweight foods that may be found at the supermarket include cocoa, instant oatmeal, granola, powdered milk, and various dried fruits.

Kitchen Equipment

In addition to carrying your food you will also have to pack some equipment for preparing the meals you will be enjoying on the trail.

If you're planning on taking a two-man, three-day trip you should make sure you've got enough food. Freeze-dried, prepackaged goods are light, convenient, and take up little room in the pack compared to other foods. Unfortunately, they're expensive, especially when you use them as your only sources of nourishment.

Since most trail food requires only the addition of boiling water, the equipment needed is simple: a stove, one or two pots, a cup, a spoon, a knife, fuel and fuel bottle, matches, canteen, and funnel or Canedy pouring cap.

A stove may seem like an extravagant and unnecessary item at first but consider what is involved if you don't carry a stove. Modern man has grown accustomed to the kitchen range with heat that can be regulated. Camp fires can be a royal pain in the hip belt; first you have to gather fire wood, then fashion some type of stone fireplace or pit, build a fire, constantly stoke it with more fuel, dodge the smoke and, while cooking or boiling water, you must give the fire and meal the kind of attention that can only come from a three-armed, asbestos-fingered aberration of what a hiker should be. In addition, fires, by their very nature, scorch the earth and cause the wilderness to be raped of wood.

The shelves of your local supermarket are filled with lightweight foods that are ideal for backpacking. All you have to do is repackage them into plastic bags once you have planned out your meals. This can save you a good deal of money over buying everything in freeze-dried, prepackaged meals. You might be able to save enough to buy a couple of special meals.

Of course a campfire adds warmth and a special type of romantic glow to any camp. When conditions permit, or in some types of survival situation, a fire is a pleasant and comforting addition. But for almost all of your cooking it makes more sense to rely on a small backpacking stove.

There are at least 30 different backpacking stoves on the market. Some have been around for years and have established reputations while others are a company's shot at the growing equipment market. Fuel ranges from alcohol to white gas and includes kerosene, bottled propane, and butane. Some of the stoves are highly efficient at boiling water, which is all that is needed to prepare most freeze-dried meals. Cold weather, altitude, freshness of the fuel, and pressure in the fuel tank all affect the efficiency of the stove.

A stove that runs on white gas (Coleman fuel) is the best bet for most types of hiking. There is no guessing as to how much fuel is left to burn as there is with bottled propane or butane stoves. White gas is easy to obtain throughout the United States and is less affected by cold weather.

A well-stocked backpacking kitchen should include these items: a bottle of fuel; some kind of canteen (metal or plastic); nesting pots for cooking, storing, and serving; knife, spoon, and cup; and, of course, a stove.

The Svea is probably the most popular backpacking stove on the market and there are several reasons for its popularity. It is compact, almost indestructible, and boils a quart of water in less than six minutes. It holds 4 ounces of fuel that will keep it running, full blast, for around an hour. The cover of the Svea can be pressed into service as a cup and the stove fits nicely inside the nesting pots carried by many backpackers.

Most white gas stoves operate in the same manner. First, the stove is filled with fuel from the fuel bottle. This can be easily accomplished with the aid of a funnel or a Canedy pouring cap that fits the top of a standard Sigg fuel bottle. (Incidentally, if you cannot find a Canedy pouring cap at your local hiking shop you can buy one directly, for $1.25, from S. Buck Canedy, P.O. Box 1685, Fall River, Mass. 02722.)

After the stove has been filled it must be primed so pressure will build up inside the fuel tank and force gas out of the tiny nozzle to be burned. To prime a Svea, put a few drops of fuel in the little indentation on the fuel tank where the generator joins. Then, light the small puddle of fuel. The burning will heat up the tank and generator and the heat will cause some of the fuel in the tank to expand. Just before

There will be times when you'll have to melt snow for your water supply. And it's at these times that you'll want a backpacking stove with good fire power and a large fuel tank. And don't forget to pack along extra fuel.

Two of the most popular backpacking stoves are the Svea 123 (left) and the Optimus 8R (right). Both burn white gas and are dependable, light in weight, and easy to operate.

the priming flame dies, turn on the stove and the fuel vapor from the tank will be ignited by the flame. The stove will now run for as long as there is fuel in the tank.

Priming takes some practice and there are many different ways of doing it, but once you have the general idea you will be able to light your stove quickly, any time of the year, and under almost all conditions. In fact, as you become more familiar with the operation of your stove, you will probably develop your own way of priming.

If you decide that you can't be bothered with all of the priming and hocus-pocus that is involved with stoves that run on white gas, you may want to buy a stove that runs on butane. One good model is the Bleuet S-2000. The Bleuet has been around for quite some time and it is one of the most reliable stoves on the market. But it does have some drawbacks. The major problem arises from the fact that once the butane cartridge has been attached, it cannot be removed until all of the fuel has been burned. Cooking on the Bleuet can be somewhat of a challenge because the height of the stove (8½ inches) requires delicate balancing. Another thing to consider is that you must do something with the empty butane canisters. Theoretically, all canisters should be

carried out but, unfortunately, you see thousands of canisters that have
been pitched off into the bush.

A good pot or two, with cover, is necessary for most types of cooking
on the trail. As with stoves, many different types of pots are on the
market. There are a few things to look for when shopping for pots that
will make the difference between a set that will last for years and a set
that will end up at the dump after a few trips. Quality backpacking
pots are made from spun aluminum rather than stamped aluminum.
A strong locking handle should be attached and the cover should fit
tightly. As a rule, the pots made in Europe are better quality than
those made in the Orient. I have had a set of Sigg nesting kettles with
wide strap bail handles that have been through all kinds of abuse.
They look and work as well now as they did eight years ago when they
were new. In addition, my Svea 123 stove fits inside the nesting pots
for a compact arrangement.

Compactness is an important consideration when you are shopping for a
backpacking stove. Some of the smaller ones fit inside the nesting pots—a
feature that will save you a good amount of pack space.

Of course you're not expected to bring your best silver on a trip. Neither should you be thinking of bringing a complete service for one. A table spoon, Sierra cup, and knife are the major tools on the trail.

Other kitchen tools include a cup, tablespoon, and pocketknife. A cup of known capacity is more important than you may think since most freeze-dried meals require a specific number of ounces of water to rehydrate. With these tools and the pot/stove combination, it is a snap to whip up a meal in a matter of minutes.

A Day on the Trail

It may be helpful to those of you just starting out backpacking to describe a typical day's eating on the trail.

Breakfast
After a good night's sleep in the bush your internal furnace needs to be stoked with enough food to get you going. As with most trail cooking, the meal begins with boiling water. While the water is approach-

ing the boiling point, I complete such preliminary camp-breaking
chores as airing my sleeping bag and taking down the tent. Then I eat
my morning meal, which usually consists of freeze-dried coffee, two
packages of instant oatmeal with a handful of raisins added, a few trail
crackers, and possibly a stick or two of beef jerky.

After breakfast, lunch items are removed from the daily food bag
and transferred to a side pocket in the pack where they will be easy to
reach later on. Then all kitchen items that will not be needed until the
evening meal are stowed inside the pack. Up goes the pack and off I go
down the trail.

While walking or during periodic rests I drink water from a canteen
that is clipped to my hip belt. I probably drink around three quarts of
water a day while on the trail, even more on hot, dry days. In most
wilderness areas fresh water is usually available, and I replenish my
canteen from some of the hundreds of fresh water springs along the
trails. If ever in doubt as to the potability of the water, I drop two
halazone tablets into every quart and let them dissolve for 30 minutes
before drinking. Because of my strong dislike for the taste of halazone,
I always add some fruit juice crystals to treated water.

Should mid-morning pangs of hunger start to rumble I take the edge
off by munching on either hard candy or gorp.

"Gorp" is a term that describes almost any mixture of fruit, nuts,
grain, and sweeteners. There are probably 500 different recipes for
gorp and now one company (Rich-Moor) has come out with a packaged variety. My favorite recipe is the following:

    1 pound M & M's solid chocolate
    1 pound mixed nuts
    1 pound raisins
    1 pound box Granola
    1 cup shredded coconut

After mixing all ingredients in a large bowl, divide the mixture into
one-cup quantities and place in plastic bags. I find that I have no
problem finishing a one-cup bag of gorp each day. I have never really
figured out how many calories are contained in a cup of gorp but I
would estimate that each cup contains at least 600 calories.

If gorp, any kind, isn't your idea of a trail snack you might try Hi-
Energy shirt pocket foods, currently marketed by Chuck Wagon. Each

1½-ounce bar contains 150 calories. Other alternatives include any of the trail snacks offered for sale at local hiking shops, candy bars (watch out for melting chocolate in the summer), beef jerky, or just about anything else you can think of that might suit your fancy while you're out on the trail.

Lunch

I find it a hassle to drag out the stove and pot to boil water, so most of my lunches, if they can be called that, consist of either a small can of tuna fish or a small can of sardines, crackers, a fruit drink, and, possibly, a piece or two of beef jerky. I'm not sure why I include canned fish for lunch while on the trail because I could just as easily carry some type of lightweight food. On occasion, when I am hiking with at least two other people, we carry a jar of peanut butter and a jar of jam. The extra weight isn't all that much and I find that the canned or jarred foods are a pleasant break from freeze-dried foods.

After lunch, it's back on the trail. Again, if any rumbling should start inside my stomach I quiet it down by munching on gorp or some other type of trail snack.

Dinner

A typical dinner on the trail consists of soup, beef Stroganoff, crackers, a fruit drink, and ice cream. The total weight of the meal, before adding water, is under 10 ounces because all of the items are freeze-dried. Three cups (24 ounces) of boiling water is required for the meal, so I begin by firing up the Svea and placing a pot of water on the stove. When the water boils I pour one cup into an empty Sierra cup and add a packet of soup mix. The remaining water in the cook pot receives the beef Stroganoff mixture that has to simmer for eight to ten minutes. While I wait for the Stroganoff to simmer I drink the soup. Just about the time I finish the soup, the main meal is ready.

After dinner a few camp chores have to be attended to. Before taking your dirty dishes down to the stream or lake side and throwing them in, think for a minute. The water in wilderness areas is, in most cases, pure. In an effort to keep it that way, it is now a common custom to do no dishwashing within 100 feet of any body of water. Take a few canteens or empty pots down to the water and fill them, then move away from the water and do the washing. If we all do this, maybe the pure waters of wilderness areas will remain pure.

This might be a good time to mention what to do with trash. I mean the food wrappers, aluminum packaging and cans, and anything else that has no value after use. There is only one thing to do with trash—*pack it out*. A popular rule is: "Leave nothing but footprints."

After the kitchen equipment has been cleaned and stowed away except for what will be needed for the morning meal, remove from the main food bag all of the items required for the next day's meals and put them into the daily food bag. It makes camp life much simpler and saves a lot of time to have all of one day's rations in one bag while the food for the rest of the trip stays in a larger bag inside the pack.

The main food bag contains several things that are important. In addition to all of the planned meals for the trip as well as fruit drink mixes and trail munchies, I also include powdered milk, salt and pepper, margarine, scrub pad (for pots), biodegradable soap (liquid), matches, sugar packets, toilet paper, halazone tablets, and emergency rations.

It may seem unnecessary to carry emergency rations, but I think a little insurance against the unexpected is in the category of good planning rather than paranoia. For several years I carried an extra day's meals to cover emergencies, but found that they never got used. Now I carry the Woodsman's Emergency Kit marketed by Chuck Wagon. The kit weighs only a few ounces and is sealed in a small waterproof box. Inside the kit are items that will sustain me temporarily if I'm ever "delayed, injured, lost, or isolated by fire, flood, or storm." The kit contains pemmican, chocolate, sucrose candy tablets, fire starter, waterproof matches, emergency compass, razor blades, and a few other goodies.

If I were to plan an emergency kit it would contain a telephone, long-range loran, rockets, yellow smoke canisters, a doctor, and for extended trips a mini-helicopter with a 200-mile range. If you really want to be prepared for an emergency, these items are essential; anything else is just spittin' in the wind.

Planning the food and cooking equipment needed for a trip into the wilderness requires a knowledge of what you like or would like to eat while on the trail. But you must be practical. On short trips you have lots of leeway, but on longer excursions you almost have to stick with freeze-dried foods. Your first step should be to send for catalogs from several of the major lightweight food manufacturers to see what kinds of foods are available.

During your trip make mental notes about your eating habits while on the trail. Are you still hungry after meals, do you feel a kind of queasiness in your stomach when you look at gorp, and how do you like the taste of freeze-dried foods? When you return to civilization you should evaluate your preferences. Generally speaking, you can't go very wrong with freeze-dried foods designed for backpackers. It might be a good idea to stick with these foods initially. After you have become more proficient at hiking and the culinary arts, you might want to experiment with some of the other lightweight food possibilities waiting at the local equipment shop and supermarket.

Good hiking and good eating!

MAJOR LIGHTWEIGHT FOOD SUPPLIERS IN THE U.S.

Chuck Wagon Foods
Micro Drive
Woburn, Massachusetts 01801

Thirty years old, over the counter and mail order, large selection

Dri Lite Foods, Inc.
11333 Atlantic
Lynwood, California 90262

Since 1951, mail order, 22 main-course meals

National Packaged Trail Foods
18607 St. Clair
Cleveland, Ohio 44110

Twenty main-course meals, chart of nutritional information, reasonable prices, mail order

Natural Food Backpack Dinners
P.O. Box 532
Corvallis, Oregon 97330

Vegetarian dinners that are great, mail order

Oregon Freeze Dry Foods, Inc.
P.O. Box 1048
Albany, Oregon 97321

The largest, with a new line of freeze-dried foods, mostly over the counter but will fill mail orders

Perma-Pak Company
(Camplite Line)
40 East 2430 South
Salt Lake City, Utah 84115

Since 1953, fair prices and good chow, mail order

Rich-Moor Corporation
P.O. Box 2728
Van Nuys, California 91494

Vast selection, mostly sells through retail outlets

Stow-A-Way Sports Industries   Largest in the East with a
166 Cushing Highway (Route 3A)   special resupply by mail
Cohasset, Massachusetts 02025   program, mail order

PART II

What You Need to Know

7

Physical Conditioning

by Dave Engerbretson

Most backpackers are "planners" who find almost as much pleasure in planning and preparing for a trip as in actually taking it. We scour catalogs in search of the ultimate in lightweight gear, and go to practically any extreme in our never ending attempt to pare the weight of our loads to the minimum. We spend countless hours pouring over maps planning trips that might never be taken, and many winter evenings are devoted to cleaning, repairing, or just tinkering with our accumulation of equipment.

By the time spring rolls around, our excitement runs high as menus are planned for the first trip, packs are loaded, and all the gear is given one last check. At long last, everything is as ready as it will ever be. Or is it?

You're not ready at all if you've forgotten to prepare the most important piece of equipment—your own body. Unfortunately, the most vital component of the entire system is often the most neglected. Your heart, lungs, blood vessels, and muscles make up the power plant that must take you into the wilderness, help you survive, and bring you home again. There can be no breakdowns, for there are no service stations to repair burned-out power plants in the backcountry. The best equipment money can buy is of little value if *you* are not physically prepared to carry it in all kinds of weather over all types of terrain.

But, again, the preparations can be fun, and the rewards are great. A physically fit backpacker will find the hills a little less steep, the loads a little lighter, and the wilderness experience more vivid when the view isn't shrouded in a cloud of fatigue.

Before you can develop a program of physical fitness to meet your own unique needs, you must understand what is meant by the term "physical fitness." There are many different definitions, but the one I like is this: *physical fitness is having the ability to get through your normal daily living routine without undue fatigue, and with enough reserve capacity to meet unforeseen emergencies.*

According to this definition, it is obvious that every individual has unique fitness needs. The level of fitness required by a professional football player, a 50-year-old banker, a 28-year-old housewife, and a 13-year-old student are all different. Thus, it may not be possible to set some rather arbitrary standards that must be met before you can be declared "physically fit."

In today's society, the level of fitness required to proceed through our daily living routine is really very low despite the mental stress and strain we all encounter. Perhaps the most important part of the definition, then, is the last part. We need sufficient reserve capacity to meet unforeseen emergencies. To the body, a weekend tennis match or ski trip, a few flights of stairs when the elevator breaks down, or a long walk when you're out of gas or can't find a parking place are all physiological emergencies. The act of backpacking itself represents an emergency situation, and, due to the nature of the activity, the potential exists for even more serious emergencies if you become lost, stranded, or injured. Your chosen form of recreation demands a large energy reserve to meet these physiological emergencies; it demands a high degree of physical fitness if the activity is to be safe and enjoyable.

According to some exercise physiologists, physical fitness is made up of six unique components: strength, flexibility, balance, agility, power, and endurance. To be considered "totally fit," a person must be fit in each of these areas.

Strength is the ability to use the muscles to generate a large force, and is measured by lifting, pulling, pushing, etc. *Flexibility* relates to the range of motion of body joints, and *balance* to the ability to maintain the body's equilibrium in a variety of unstable positions. *Agility* is the ability to change gross body positions rapidly, while *power* is the rate of doing work, i.e., how fast you can use your strength. *Endurance*

Muscular strength is developed through such exercises as weight lifting. Exercises designed to increase the strength of the legs and back are particularly important in backpacking.

is the ability to perform a movement repeatedly over a long period of time. It may refer to either the muscles or to the cardiovascular system —the heart and blood vessels.

A person who backpacks as a recreational activity may need a moderately high fitness level in each of these six components. But how do you obtain fitness in each of these areas? Simply stated, you get what you train for. That is, if you want to improve your strength, you must do strength exercises; if you want flexibility, do flexibility exercises, and so on. This is the reason why a weight-lifting program or a jogging program, or any other program with a single focus, will not produce all-round fitness. It's a simple fact: To become "totally fit," a person must perform exercises that require each specific fitness component.

In addition, these exercises must be done according to the "Overload Principle," which states that a body system must be stressed over and above its normal load if it is to improve its level of function. In other words, if your daily work normally calls for you to lift 50-pound bags of flour, you will develop the strength required to perform this task.

To develop flexibility, exercises should be done which require the muscles to stretch and the joints to move through their full range of motion. By increasing flexibility you lessen the chances of pulling a muscle during a strenuous hike.

But you will not become stronger unless you subject the muscles involved to loads in excess of 50 pounds for a given length of time.

Although all six of the fitness components are of some importance to the backpacker, cardiovascular endurance is unquestionably the major factor in backpacking success. The cardiovascular system—the heart and blood vessels—provides the means of transportation for moving fuel, oxygen, and wastes to and from the working muscles. While there are many physiological benefits to be derived from a high degree of cardiovascular fitness, for the backpacker it means that heavy loads can be packed up hill and down for an extended period of time with less fatigue. A person simply must have a reasonably high level of cardiovascular fitness to be a successful backpacker.

The problem is how to achieve the cardiovascular fitness required for backpacking. The solution is simple: If you want endurance, you must do exercises that require endurance, and you must subject your

Another key component of physical fitness is balance. By practicing a variety of stunts, such as walking on a rail, you'll improve your body's ability to maintain its equilibrium in a variety of unstable positions.

own cardiovascular system to loads in excess of your usual activity level.

There are a number of methods for doing this, but some are more effective than others in producing optimal results. The program I like is called Continuous Rhythmical Interval Progressive Endurance training—C-R-I-P-E. Most people simply call it interval training. But I like the longer name because once the title is understood, the entire program is also understood.

The CRIPE theory applies to everyone—to a teen-ager, a business executive, a housewife, or a senior citizen. The theory applies to all; the difference, as you will see, is how it's applied.

What is your idea of a good fitness program? Tennis? Handball? Jogging? Swimming? Each of these can be of value, but for the best cardiovascular improvement certain criteria must be met. The words in the title—CRIPE—describe these criteria.

The first word is *continuous*. No matter what exercise you do, you should do it continuously, that is, non-stop. If you plan to work out for 30 minutes or an hour, exercise the entire time. Don't exercise vigorously for ten minutes, and then sit and rest for ten before continu-

Agility is the ability to change gross body positions rapidly and can be developed by activities that require quick changes in direction such as this run through a course of pylons.

ing. Of course, unless you know the trick, it may be almost impossible for you to exercise nonstop for a significant length of time. The trick will be discussed with another of the title words.

The exercise must be a *rhythmical* one. Rhythmical exercises are those that produce smooth alternating contractions and relaxations of the muscles such as walking, jogging, cross-country skiing, swimming, rowing, or cycling. Such exercises promote the circulation of blood in contrast to exercises involving excessive muscle tension, which partially inhibit the circulation for brief periods, as in weight lifting, for example. Any of the rhythmical activities named work very well for producing improved cardiovascular fitness. Select the ones you enjoy most or the ones most convenient for you to do.

A rhythmical exercise must be done continuously, and the trick to working continuously is found in the next word—interval. Interval work is work done at varying intensities over a period of time. You work hard for a short time, then you work less hard until you recover. Then you work harder again. By alternating periods of hard and lighter work and selecting the proper intervals, work can continue for an

The cardiovascular system is the most important in the body and a healthy one is necessary no matter what activity you engage in. Cardiovascular endurance is developed by such activities as jogging, cycling, rowing, swimming, or cross-country skiing, particularly when these activities are performed over long distances.

extended period. At no time will you be completely inactive or completely exhausted.

Using jogging as an example, the proper intervals can be selected as follows. Begin jogging at a comfortable pace, and run until you begin to feel out of breath and tired, say in two blocks. Then slow to a walk until your breathing returns to normal and you have recovered. This may take one block. Then jog again. Thus, your interval is run two blocks and walk one, run two, walk one, and so on. A similar procedure would be used if you had chosen swimming, cycling, or any other rhythmical activity.

The interval nature of the exercise is the reason why this program is suitable for everyone. Each person selects the work intervals that are most appropriate for his immediate needs. The teen-ager may run ten blocks and walk one, while the senior citizen may walk one block quickly and the following one slowly, but each is doing what is right in his own case.

After following this type of program for several weeks, you will discover that you are no longer tired at the end of your usual interval of hard work, and you are recovering before the end of your "rest" interval. Your body has adapted to the overload, and the next word in the title—*progressive*—must be considered. It has become time to increase the work level in order to continue to apply an overload to the cardiovascular system. That is, it's time to progress to a new interval. This can be done by lengthening the work period or shortening the rest period, or both. Care should be taken, though, to only increase the load by a small amount each time. If your interval has been run two/walk one, for example, change it to run three/walk one. Don't try to increase it to run ten/walk one. This will produce too much of an overload, and your body may not be able to make the adjustment. It is far better to make many small progressions of the work interval rather than two or three large adjustments.

The final word in the title, *endurance*, merely indicates that you are taking part in a physical conditioning program that requires and develops endurance. Endurance means distance. Therefore it is best to increase the work load by increasing the distance run (or swam, or cycled, etc.), rather than by increasing the speed of the work.

A program such as this can produce significant improvements in cardiovascular fitness (endurance) if followed three times per week for approximately 45 to 60 minutes each time. Initially, if you're in poor

Power is the rate of doing work, or the speed with which you can use your strength. It is developed by activities such as jumping or, in this case, running up flights of stairs.

condition, it may be necessary to start with workouts of shorter duration and gradually lengthen them over a period of time. As your condition begins to improve, you may work out every day if you desire, but initially it is probably best to rest a day between each exercise period.

How hard you should work each time is best left up to you. You should work hard enough to be tired when you are finished. If you're not, you probably haven't done enough to make any difference. On the other hand, you should recover quickly, and by the time you have showered and dressed you should feel good If you don't, and your workout exhausts you for the rest of the day, you did too much and should reduce your intervals the next time.

That's part of the beauty of this type of conditioning program. Each individual determines the pace, interval, and work load that is correct for him, and each progresses at his own rate.

And, remember, as you adapt to a given work load you must progress to increasingly more difficult intervals if you are to continue to improve your fitness. But, of course, you don't keep progressing indefinitely. When you reach a level that feels right to you, stay there. The adequacy of your level of fitness will make itself known on your first backpacking trip!

A well-trained cardiovascular system isn't the only type of fitness you'll need for backpacking, though. You will recall that there are five other factors included under the term "total fitness." Of these, strength is probably the next most important for a backpacker, but conditioning for any of them can easily be incorporated into the CRIPE exercise program.

After determining which other areas of your fitness require improvement, simply incorporate exercises for these areas into your regular CRIPE intervals. In the case of strength, for example, run/walk two of your normal intervals and then do strength exercises for your arms and upper body. Then repeat a couple of run/walk intervals, and do strength exercises for your legs, and so on. In the same way, exercises for flexibility, balance, or the other areas can be built into your conditioning program.

When attempting to design this part of your program, keep in mind that you must do exercises specifically for the type of fitness you are trying to improve, and you must do the exercises so they place a load on the system that is greater than the load with which they normally function. There are many good exercise books that will help you with this portion of your program, or you can design your own with the help of these principles.

A second method of developing these other types of fitness is to do the CRIPE program for cardiovascular conditioning three days per week, and exercise for the others on the alternate days. Either method is acceptable, and you should select the one that best fits your schedule.

There's another problem for backpackers: fat. Excess body fat is the backpacker's worst enemy. In addition to the cardiovascular stress resulting from the need to supply overabundant fat tissue with blood, the presence of the fat tissue itself is a limiting factor in endurance activities. Due to the sheer weight of the fat, the energy cost of almost every activity is greater for an overweight individual. If a person is 20 percent overweight, the energy cost of physical activity is increased by a similar amount. The excess fat also interferes with the body's cooling mechanisms during exercise, which places an increased burden upon the circulatory system and further reduces endurance. Then, too, the conditions that are conducive to the development of fat are the same ones leading to poor physical fitness. Is it any wonder that backpacking is difficult if you're overweight?

While a complete discussion of weight control is outside the scope of this chapter, the subject is of great importance to backpackers. Weight control is such a popular topic today that it's difficult to pick up a magazine that does not contain at least one article on some new "miracle diet" or other weight-loss method. Unfortunately, a great deal of this writing almost completely ignores the physiological principles of weight control. But these principles cannot be disregarded by anyone who hopes to accomplish a significant weight loss.

Physiologically, weight control is very simple. From a practical standpoint, of course, it's neither simple nor easy. We all know that if more calories are taken in than are burned, the excess becomes fat tissue and you gain weight. But if more calories are burned than are taken in, weight is lost. This relationship between the number of calories taken in as food and the number burned in the process of living is known as metabolic balance. Whenever there's an imbalance totaling 3,500 calories, your weight will change by one pound. To lose fat, you must eat fewer calories, burn up more, or both. If you understand this, you are on your way to a sound weight-control program.

The number of calories you use is determined by your daily activity level, and the only practical way to burn more calories is to increase your physical activity. It has been suggested by some that you must

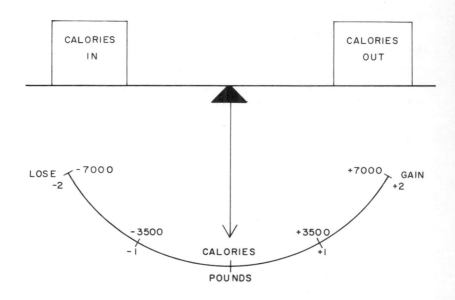

METABOLIC BALANCE

Metabolic balance is the relationship between the number of calories taken in as food and the number burned in the process of living. If you burn up 7,000 calories more than you take in, you'll lose two pounds. On the other hand, if you take in 7,000 more than you burn, the excess becomes fat tissue and you gain weight. Thus, whenever the imbalance totals 3,500 calories, your weight will change by 1 pound.

chop wood for 8 hours or walk for 12 to burn up the equivalent of a pound of fat, which makes it appear that exercise is a poor way to lose weight. This isn't exactly correct, however.

It is true that if the average caloric cost of chopping wood for several minutes is measured and this cost divided into 3,500 calories, it would appear that about 8 hours of chopping is required to lose 1 pound of fat. But this procedure does not consider the fact that as the work continues its energy cost increases, or that your metabolism does not return to its resting level as soon as the exercise stops. That is, in 60 minutes you actually burn more than 60 times the calories used in one minute of chopping, and you continue to burn calories at an elevated rate for some time after the exercise ends.

But even if it were true that you must chop wood for 8 hours to lose 1 pound of fat, no one says that this must be 8 hours of continuous chopping. If you chop wood for 1 hour every day, you will still burn the equivalent of about 46 pounds per year! The fact remains that increased physical activity is the only practical method of burning more calories.

To be really effective in burning calories, an exercise must last a fairly long time—say an hour or so. No matter how strenuous the activity, you simply cannot do enough work in a short period of time to burn a significant number of calories. In other words, an endurance-type activity is most effective as a weight loss program, and fortunately for backpackers, this is exactly the type of activity that was recommended in the CRIPE program for cardiovascular conditioning.

In addition to a formal conditioning program, it is also possible to significantly increase the number of calories burned by attempting to become more physically active throughout your entire day. Park a few extra blocks from work and walk. Take the stairs rather than the elevator, and walk to lunch rather than drive. Several hundred extra calories can easily be burned in a day with very little extra effort, and every extra calorie is a chip from another pound of fat.

On the other side of the metabolic balance, the number of calories eaten each day is as important as the number burned. That means but one thing—diet. More words have undoubtedly been written concerning dieting than about any other single topic known to man. Fad diets are legion. The water diet, the grapefruit diet, the drinking man's diet, the ski team diet, and on and on. And most of such diets work—up to a point.

The fact is, you can eat nothing but ice cream for every meal and still lose weight. If your daily living requires 2,000 calories, and you eat 1,500 calories of nothing but ice cream every day, you'll lose about a pound a week. Of course, 1,500 calories of ice cream is not very much ice cream so you'll be hungry a lot of the time; and since you will not be eating a balanced diet, you may eventually get sick. You won't be able to continue the diet indefinitely, and as soon as you go back to your old eating habits you'll gain weight again.

These, then, are some of the problems with the majority of fad diets. They are not usually well balanced in terms of protein, fat, and carbohydrates, and, therefore, are not healthy over a long period of time. In addition, being "crash diets" designed to produce rapid weight loss, they are very restrictive in terms of total caloric intake, so you feel hungry most of the time. These two conditions make it very difficult to stick to the diet and to maintain a weight loss.

For the average backpacker who is not obese but merely has a "few pounds to lose," there is a better way. I call it the "No-Diet Diet." As the name implies, this is not a diet at all, but a healthful way of eating that can save a bundle of calories at the same time. You can eat almost anything you like, you will never go hungry, and you can lose weight!

According to the title of one popular book, "Calories Don't Count." But as we have seen, calories are, in fact, the only things that do count with respect to weight loss. To lose weight, you must shift the metabolic balance so you are taking in fewer calories than you require for daily living. The goal of the "No-Diet Diet" is to show you how to do this without following a strict diet, and to allow you to develop sound eating habits that will allow you to take off excess pounds—and keep them off.

There are many ways to save calories during the day without missing them and without going hungry. Stop and consider what you ate yesterday. A piece of bread with two pats of butter? A piece of pie with two scoops of ice cream? Two spoonfuls of gravy on your mashed potatoes? A bag of potato chips with your sandwich?

These same things could have been eaten with fewer calories. Each pat of butter is worth 50 calories. Eat the bread, but use only one pat of butter, and you've saved 50 calories. Use only one scoop of ice cream on your pie and you've saved another 150 calories. Only one spoonful of gravy on your potatoes rather than two saves you approximately 50 calories. And the potato chips are real diet killers! If a potato is worth 100 calories when baked, that same potato will contain about 300 calories when french fried, and about 600 calories when prepared as potato chips. This is due, of course, to the grease used in cooking the french fries and chips. Thus, the *way* you prepare your food can also save a significant number of calories.

Try to think of other ways you could save calories in your daily diet. There are opportunities everywhere. Don't fry your meat, broil it. Use half as much jelly and butter on your morning toast. Drink diet soft drinks rather than those containing sugar. Drink two percent, low fat or skim milk instead of whole milk. Switch to a low-calorie salad dressing. Eat your potatoes baked. It's easy, and you don't really give up anything or go hungry. Make a game of it and you'll be amazed at the places you can trim calories without missing them. You're not on a diet, you are just a little thoughtful about what you eat.

Combining the "No-Diet Diet" with a plan of increased physical activity can shift the metabolic balance considerably, and result in a significant weight loss. Merely taking a little care in what you eat and how it's prepared, and avoiding the little high-calorie "munchies," you can reduce your daily intake by at least 250 calories without missing them. If you also attempt to walk more, climb more steps, and be more active in general, you can easily burn another 250 calories a day. Together that's 500 calories a day, and that's a pound a week. If you also begin a CRIPE exercise program to improve your cardiovascular endurance, you will, of course, burn even more calories, and lose even more weight.

Most backpackers are planners. And those who are serious about it take care to prepare for the rigors of the sport by keeping their weight under control and their bodies physically fit.

8

Wilderness Hygiene

by Louis V. Bignami

It's a fact of life: backpackers are never as clean on the trail as they are at home. And nowadays, the trails aren't even as clean as they used to be, thanks to the clods who leave their foil freeze-dry wrappers as calling cards. The result is that sanitation has become a major problem in the crowded sections of our backcountry.

As a backpacker your hygiene can be divided into three parts: your insides, your outsides, and your gear. Careful attention to each of these areas will keep you comfortable and healthy in the field. A slapdash approach, whether from unconcern or a lack of knowledge, will quickly foul up your trip. If trying to stay warm in dirty or sweat-soaked gear hasn't already changed your sleep to shivers, digestive problems surely will and constipation or "the runs" will make your life miserable. Fortunately, these problems are relatively easy to overcome.

Perhaps the biggest problem afield these days is water and its diminution in quality. It used to be that you could drink at any wilderness stream and suffer no ill effects. But now, far too many slobs are using our streams as open toilets and stinking kitchen sinks. In many areas of the country all streams are suspect, and even in the vastness of the western mountains you'll do well to drink from streams above meadows and popular campsites.

Babbling brooks seem to be bubbling detergent everywhere, and crossroads mountain meadow camps have bacteria counts that would

We should all be striving to keep our wilderness areas clean—for our own
personal health and for the health of our natural environment. In far too
many areas of the country all streams are suspect, thanks to detergent use and
human waste by thoughtless wilderness travelers.

be more appropriate to urban slum sewers. So you should be prepared to take some steps. Maybe the English had the right idea. Some historians feel that the reason the British were able to thrive in the tropics while other nationalities were dropping like flies was due to a combination of fastidious personal cleanliness and the drinking of large amounts of tea. If you're a tea drinker, you won't have to worry much about water quality. Hot tea with meals is most refreshing, and cold tea is a delight when chugging up sunbaked switchbacks. Plastic canteens seem to be required here though, for tea sometimes does strange things to metal containers.

If this doesn't appeal, then you should carry water-purification tablets. Halazone tablets are a time-tested standard, and they're both cheap and very light. One hundred weigh less than half an ounce and one will usually be enough to purify a pint of water. Just drop it in, give the canteen a few shakes, wait a half hour, and you're protected. Really grungy water might require two tablets.

In case you don't care for the chlorine taste that the halazone tablets give the water, you can improve things somewhat by pouring half a canteen of water into an open pot and letting it stand for a half hour more. The hour's delay between the time the tablet is dropped into the water and the time you can drink the water may be a problem. If you're really thirsty, and only carry a single canteen, you may not be able to wait. My solution is to carry two canteens and as soon as either one runs out I refill it. If the water still tastes funny to you after all this, you can add any of a number of powdered fruit drinks.

If you pack much in desert country, or where thermal springs or mineral springs are common, you've got to be especially careful. These water sources can have dangerous natural additives—like arsenic—so all bitter-tasting springs should be avoided.

The absence of animal tracks around water and of insect life in water can be a warning of a bubbling bucolic Borgia. Incidentally, you're *very* foolish if you walk into the desert without at least consulting a good book on desert survival. Most "desert rats" know that several extra canteens of water are usually preferable to an equal amount of food and other gear. In some sections of the Southwest, four or more quart canteens aren't excessive.

If you're packing into high country, where the water is still unspoiled spring water or snow melt, you're going to have to be careful not to drink too much when you're overheated. If you lap up too much cold water when you reach that tinkling spring at the end of a long,

If you're backpacking in high altitudes, where the water is still unspoiled springs or simply snow melt, be careful not to drink too much when you're overheated. You could end up with cramps or, even worse, the runs.

dry scramble, you're likely to drop the temperature of your stomach and get a case of the cramps. You can also get a super case of the runs.

Wherever you backpack you may find that the combination of unaccustomed exercise and strange water will give you a case of stop-and-goes. Prunes and cheese are natural remedies for this, and drugstore remedies can be purchased. If this is a persistent problem, it's a good sign that a trip to your family doctor may be needed. He can check over your plumbing and give you a prescription for field use.

Ladies in the outdoors have their own special problems. Menstrual cycles aren't always reliable when the woman's body is subjected to a big change in altitude and energy expenditures. If your period doesn't come on schedule, don't panic. This is another relatively common effect of altitude change.

Since drugstores aren't available in the backcountry, you should bring along a sufficient supply of whatever you regularly use. Most lady hikers prefer tampons to prevent chaffing.

If you keep your insides in reasonable order you can start to think about your outside. Staying clean consists mostly of a state of mind and a little care. Minimum conditions depend on your situation. Honeymoon backpackers obviously require a higher state of cleanliness than an all-male fishing trip. One sure way to stay clean is to share a double bag. You can be certain you smell at least as bad as your partner, and this can encourage baths like nothing else.

Actually there are two major systems for keeping clean in the outdoors. Either you can take the piecemeal approach or you can wait until everything stinks and do a personal urban renewal project. The first method is preferred because, as in most outdoor situations, it's easier to attack a minor problem before it becomes a major one.

If you take a daily maintenance approach, staying clean is a snap if you don't try and wash up after dark or so early in the morning that you're cracking ice off the edge of your water bucket. All you really need is a hotel-size bar of soap (or a half bar of any standard size) and a washcloth or bandanna, and you're in business. Just keep these in an outside pocket of your pack where you don't have to dig for them.

During warm days, when you're hiking in shorts and T-shirt, you can give your arms and legs a damp wash during your trail breaks. If you're going shirtless you should also wash the rest of your torso—especially your back. There's nothing that feels so good as a quick, cold swipe of a wet cloth on your back when you've been carrying a pack. This is even more true if you've got a frameless pack.

In desert areas you can accomplish this with very little water. You may even use the water to rinse out your mouth first before using it on your bandanna. This won't hurt the cooling effect of that evaporation on your back a bit, although it's something most packers won't want to admit.

Shaving isn't really very enjoyable in the field. Most men can get away without shaving over a weekend, but then the itches set in. If you can stand this for a day or two more, you can omit shaving until you get out to the trailhead. But if you're traveling with a friendly lady, you'll probably want to take steps not to let a sprouting beard cause uncomfortable friction. There are several reasonable solutions; for example, one of the new disposable razors will give you reasonable shaves if you soak your face in warm water. A windup razor from a mountain shop may be a better solution if you're used to an electric shaver. There are also several types of battery razors that will give you a week's shaves. Rechargeable shavers work, too, but most are pretty heavy. A shaving mirror will come in handy here, although aluminum foil or the shiny bottom of a cup will serve in a pinch.

With the use of breaks to tidy up you'll find that major cleaning in evening camps will be much easier and quicker. Still it's important to note that an early stop on washdays is a big plus. This is especially true in cold weather. If it's really cold, a good trick is to keep your bottom half clothed while you wash the top. Then put on clean shirts, etc., and strip your bottom part for cleaning. This makes it reasonably easy to wash and still keep warm.

You also could buy a Sunshower, a nifty gadget that weighs only 12 ounces, and is, in effect, a solar-powered shower that uses sunlight to heat the 2½-gallon plastic bag. This lets you use the sun for a couple or three hours during the afternoon to get water hot enough for a great shower. And you can use the excess for dishwashing. It also is an answer to the water carrying and holding problem in camp. At $9.95

Weighing just 12 ounces, the Sunshower can give you 2½ gallons of warm water for showering or cleaning dishes.

from Basic Designs, Box 287, Muir Beach, Sausalito, California, it's a good deal.

If you're really hardy you can swim in high country lakes. Try to find a spot with a light, shallow, sandy bottom as this is usually the warmest water—particularly if it's near the outlet. Though skinny dipping is traditional and jockey shorts will do in an emergency, a racing suit is a good choice. It will also give you something to wear when you're washing the rest of your gear. *Warning*: skinny dipping at high altitudes can give you the burn of your life in the worst possible areas, so take care!

Aside from general bathing you should pay particular care to your feet. Many backpackers feel that washing the feet merely softens them. But keeping the feet clean and dry is an absolute must. Alcohol rubs and rinses—carry the alcohol in a small (2-ounce) squeeze bottle—will help you toughen and cool your feet at the same time. This type of rub also feels great on your back when you're packing a frameless pack without a shirt.

Blisters develop when abrasion between your skin and your socks heats up the tissue. So careful washing and alcohol rubs really can help here. Some people find foot powder useful, too. If you change to clean dry socks during breaks, you can improve your chances for maintaining comfortable feet.

Perhaps the most dangerous, and certainly the most disgusting, group of outdoor people are the backpackers who haven't learned to deal with john problems in a safe and sanitary manner. Starting to set up camp in an ideal location, only to realize that there's a funny smell in the air and your site has been used for a john, isn't particularly amusing. And stepping barefoot into someone else's feces is even less amusing. Waste elimination should be simple in almost any site. In the desert there's no real problem as you just bury waste in a small hole after burning the toilet paper with a match. Be sure to restore the rock cover you've displaced to prevent wind erosion from uncovering your deposit.

In mountainous areas of the West you should take special care to get out of meadows where there are a lot of campers. A short trip up to drier ground is called for, and you should never use a likely campsite for a john. A spot in the brush or an area in rocks where there's not enough level ground to pitch a tent is always your best choice. Using overhanging rockshelter areas for toilets is not recommended, as these areas are likely spots for campsites in foul weather.

Waste eliminations should be simple in almost any site. In the desert, or any nonsnowy region, you can dig a hole, bury your waste and then restore the rock cover or a good amount of soil. Just be sure to dig deep enough so that wind erosion won't uncover your deposit, and be sure to dig well away from any water source.

Always be sure to pick a spot for your personal latrine that is well away from streams, and downstream from campsites, if possible. This will give the earth a chance to naturally filter out wastes.

Backpacking during early-season snows presents its own special problems. If you bury wastes in snow you can imagine what's going to happen when that snow melts. In this situation you just have to try to do the best you can. Meltholes around trees can provide you with the chance to bury your wastes in the usual "cat hole." If the snow's too deep for this, at least get off the trail.

Giving your hands a rinse after you make a john call is obviously a good idea and you can take a canteen, a washcloth, some matches for burning toilet paper, and a cake of soap along with you in order to stay reasonably clean. In the desert, or where there's a water problem, you can do a fair job of washing your hands by rubbing them with clean dry sand.

If you have sufficient water and take the time, there should be no problem keeping your body clean. But you also have to keep your clothing and cooking gear clean enough so you will be comfortable and not subject to those various internal problems that can result from dirty mess gear. All cooking equipment should be cleaned with bio-degradable detergent, but plain old soap also works well and you can use the same bar for you, your clothing, and your equipment.

The first rule, however, is not to wash dishes, clothing, or yourself in any stream. If you do, you're adding to the water quality problem. So to get water to where the action should be, you must invest in a plastic folding bucket or that Sunshower mentioned earlier.

Cooking gear is easy to keep clean if you add water to pots as they empty. Metal or plastic scrubbing pads, or even a pine cone, make good scrubbing brushes. The secret here is to use only enough water to get a film of soap on things. Then use a single warm or hot rinse. Don't dispose of waste water by throwing it in camp. Most cleaning water has food particles in it and will eventually attract flies and smell. Taking the time to move your cleanup to a spot that is less likely to be used than your campsite is worth the effort and only takes a few extra minutes. If you realize that a lot—some of my doctor buddies feel most—of the various sicknesses that are usually lumped under "mountain sickness" are really the result of bad hygiene, then you'll probably take the care that you should in this area.

Clean clothes aren't a problem if you're only out for the weekend. You can pack a change and the smell won't get to you until you're back at the car on your way home. On longer trips a layover day every four or five days is recommended. This gives you a chance to air your sleeping bag, tidy up your tent, and wash some clothes.

Plain soap will do the job here if you use some elbow grease to rub up a good lather. A mild detergent such as Ivory is my soap recommendation, and if you want lots of suds you can make a reasonable imitation of soap flakes by using a pocket knife to make shavings.

The same cautions about spreading soapy water around camp and into streams apply here. Note also that if there are porcupines in the area you'll be wise to put your soap in a spot where they can't feast on it. Hang clothing that is to be left out all night high enough so they won't eat that either. Sweat-stained clothing also has a fatal attraction to those little beasties, so hang it in a tree along with your pack.

Socks are an important enough part of your outdoor wardrobe to deserve special attention. Ragg socks are the pro's choice, and these should be cleaned with plain soap. Many backpackers change their socks at their noon break and give the dirty pair a quick wash and a

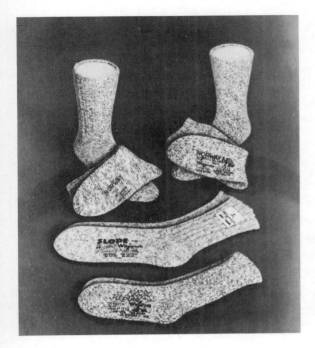

Socks are a vital part of your backpacking gear. You should always bring enough pairs so that you can change frequently, as many as three times a day. A good quality Ragg sock will minimize foot care problems and make rinsing and drying easier.

rinse. Then they wring them out and dry them on the top of their pack as they chug along the trail. A pair of clothespins can come in handy here as drying socks have a way of falling off the pack, and you may find yourself backtracking to find that lost sock. The pins are also handy for hanging wash in camp.

If you really get hot around noon, a change of underwear can be most refreshing. Lots of foot powder applied on your feet and wherever else it'll do you some good is a fine idea.

About all that's left to do is to clean your sleeping bag liner if you use one. Most find that these are a great idea since you can't readily wash a down or synthetic-filled bag in the field. On hot days, or nights, you can use your bag for a pad and sleep in the liner, and liners certainly will increase the useful life for your bag by keeping it clean. Cotton liners also feel better than nylon, and cut down that "bag smell" that some find so objectionable. Give one a try, or make one, and you'll probably never be without one in the field.

Clearly, staying clean and reasonably hygienic in the field is easier as you grow more experienced and learn what is going to make a mess. A pilgrim trying to cook on an open fire can make an awful mess of pots and hands, while a camp chef can do the same job and have most of the mess cleaned up before dinner is served.

The same holds true for gear. Good gear doesn't get as dirty as inexpensive stuff, and experienced climbers or backpackers stay out of the spots that are going to get them filthy. But you will find that the real division between clean and comfortable backpackers and those that look—and scratch—like a skid row bums is just a little extra care when cleaning problems are small. The backpacker's world is much too fine to be sick in.

9

How to Pack a Pack

by Martin Hanft

How well you pack your backpack can be important. Just as important is knowing what to take with you when you go. Sixty pounds of camping equipment, no matter how well it's packed, will always weigh 60 pounds.

A lot of people seem to be have forgotten that the purpose of hiking is to get out into the woods. Whether you hike to fish for trout in a mountain lake, to hunt for quail, or just for the pleasure of walking through the woods, the enjoyment stems from the woods you find around you, not from the load on your back. Time spent fretting over a heavy pack is time lost enjoying the hike. Remember: keep it light.

The way I keep my backpack light is by making a list of all the equipment I might ever reasonably want to take with me into the woods, and then I go down the list to see what I won't need *on this particular trip*. I go down the list a second time and cross off everything I can do without but didn't have the courage to cross off the first time. I've found that any number of supposedly "indispensable" items rarely, if ever, leave the pack.

This is my equipment checklist. Bearing in mind the time of year, the trail conditions I expect to find, and the length of the trip I'm planning, I pare this list down to the bare essentials. Then I pack the items I haven't crossed off and head out for the trail.

Checklist of Backpacking Gear

_____ Bandanna
_____ Body/foot powder
_____ Book (reading material)
_____ Camera and film
_____ Candles and candle holder
_____ Can opener
_____ Canteen (s)
_____ Clothing (extra)
_____ Compass
_____ Cup
_____ Eating utensils
_____ First-aid box
_____ Flashlight, extra batteries, and bulb
_____ Food
_____ Gaiters
_____ Ground sheet
_____ Hat
_____ Ice axe
_____ Ice creepers
_____ Insect repellent
_____ Knife
_____ Maps
_____ Match box
_____ Mattress or foam pad
_____ Memo book
_____ Mittens
_____ Needle and thread
_____ Pen or pencil
_____ Poncho
_____ Pot lifter
_____ Pots
_____ Razor
_____ Saw
_____ Shirt
_____ Shoes (extra) and/or booties
_____ Snake-bite kit

_____ Snowshoes
_____ Soap
_____ Soap pads
_____ Socks
_____ Stove and extra fuel
_____ Sunglasses
_____ Suntan oil
_____ Sweatband
_____ Sweater
_____ Tent and tent pegs
_____ Tent broom (for winter camping)
_____ Thermometer
_____ Toilet paper
_____ Towel
_____ Trash can liners
_____ Underwear
_____ Washcloth
_____ Water bottle
_____ Water-purification tablets

Some General Tips for Packing

The most important thing to remember while packing your bag is to try to keep the heavier items in the pack as high and as close as possible to the packframe. The ideal situation—at least in terms of weight distribution—would be to carry all of the weight of the pack directly above the shoulders. Weight carried high and close to the body has the least tendency to drag down the hiker by pulling him backwards. In the Adirondack Mountains of New York, I've seen backpackers carrying loads of 100 pounds and more on wooden packframes that extend 4 feet above their shoulders. Knowing where to carry the weight makes it possible.

There should be no sharp, exposed surfaces on any of the items in the pack. The sharp edges will do an enormous amount of damage to the bag in no time at all. Such angular items as a stove, fuel bottle, or cooking pot should be arranged with a flat side toward the packframe, or padded with a sweater or extra shirt to keep them out of your back.

Emergency items—and anything else you might want to get at without unpacking—should be kept either at the top of the pack or in one

Though you may not believe it, all you see here will fit into or onto the packframe-and-bag combination. Remember to keep the heavier items as high in the pack and as close to the frame as possible.

of the outside pockets. Items such as a first-aid box, flashlight, poncho, canteen, toilet paper, and insect repellent should all be readily and quickly available.

Make sure that nothing in your pack rattles or bangs as you walk. The noise starts out as an annoyance and ends up as a nerve-jangling din. The worst offender is often a loose spoon or fork in an aluminum pot. Wrap a rubber band around your eating utensils and keep them in a pocket of your pack, protected by a plastic bag. Place padding (an extra shirt, underwear, or some wool socks) in between the large metal items in your pack, such as the stove and cook kit. Shake your pack a few times as you load your gear to check for unpleasant noises.

Don't hang, tie, or attach anything to the bottom of your pack that will swing or catch in your legs as you walk. The pack should feel sturdy and solid on your back. Any discomfort will tend to increase the longer you walk, and the pendulum motion of a frying pan tied to your pack's drawstring as an afterthought will grate on you faster than you may realize.

Pack as wide as the width of your body, never wider. You're prob-

Items that you'll be using around camp, such as candles, reading material, saw, etc., should be packed close to the frame and in the lower compartment of a two-compartment bag. Those things that you'll need quick access to should be packed far away from the frame. These items include your first-aid kit, rain poncho, extra sweater, medicated powder, insect repellent, and the like.

ably used to the width of your shoulders, and your eye will automatically tell you whether you can walk between the boulders without sidling. A tent or sleeping bag that extends out beyond your body is sure to catch on every stray branch.

Balance the weight inside your pack. Don't let one side become much heavier than the other. An unbalanced pack can grow into a big problem. It doesn't weigh any more than a balanced pack, but it feels as if it does.

Finally, decide where you'll pack your gear and then keep it there. After a few days on the trail, you'll know where everything is and you'll be comfortable with the arrangement. There's nothing so frustrating as forgetting where you packed the extra flashlight bulb, and having to take your pack apart in the dark to find it.

First Considerations—Backpack, Sleeping Bag, Tent

Backpack. Before you start thinking about what you'll pack, give a little thought to what you'll be packing it into. For years I've had two backpacks—a canvas rucksack and a sturdy frame-and-bag combination. The advantages of a rucksack are that it's light, inexpensive, and not nearly as ponderous a contraption to tie to your back as the packframe-and-bag. I use mine for anything from a day hike to a three-day excursion, and I much prefer it for all shorter trips. Better quality rucksacks have leather (sometimes padded) shoulder straps that are attached to the bag with a brass ring. Web shoulder straps, sewn directly onto the bag, have a tendency to pull free with use. Almost all rucksacks have outside pockets, and they are available in all sizes. Some rucksacks have waistbands, and a few have internal frames.

The principal advantage of the packframe-and-bag combination is that it is more comfortable for carrying heavy loads (more than 30 pounds). The reason for this is that the weight of the bag is suspended from a metal frame and doesn't press into the back of the hiker. Most packframe and bags have padded waistbands that are used to support most of the burden. Some backpackers adjust their packs so that all of the weight rests on the waistband and use the shoulder straps only to keep the pack balanced. Many packframe bags are divided into compartments for sorting the load and keeping the heavier items on top.

Although the packframe-and-bag combination has almost overshadowed the rucksack for extended backpacking trips, it does have some drawbacks. It's more expensive, it's more likely to be damaged by hard wear, and wearing one can make the hiker feel harnessed or "strapped in."

My packframe and bag is divided into two compartments—upper and lower—and it has six large outside pockets, two on the left side of the bag, two on the right, and two on the face of the bag. In addition, there is a map pocket inside the flap of the top compartment.

Sleeping bag. Although the sleeping bag is probably the heaviest item in the pack, it's not really very heavy for its size. Down-filled sleeping bags are usually the lightest for the amount of warmth they offer, and large down bags pack into surprisingly small stuff sacks.

That's an important consideration if you plan to be carrying your sleeping bag inside your pack or rucksack.

Sleeping bags stuffed with such man-made fibers as duPont Fiberfill II or Celanese Fortrel PolarGuard have advantages, too. They retain more of their warmth when wet and they're less expensive than down-filled bags. But when it comes to packing a bag into your pack, the down bags are tops.

Most sleeping bags come with stuff sacks made of waterproofed, coated nylon. The stuff sack alone—when it's new—is enough to keep your bag dry, even in a day-long rain. But coated nylon tends to deteriorate when subjected to bright sunlight and rough wear, and nothing is rougher on the stuff sack than its being tied down onto a packframe with straps, ropes, or shock cords. If your stuff sack doesn't keep your bag as dry as it should, line the inside of the stuff sack with a plastic trash bag, squeeze all of the air that you can out of the bag, and seal the plastic bag with a twist-tie. Of course, the plastic bag can be used outside the stuff sack, but then the thin plastic tends to catch on brush and branches. Used as a liner, the inexpensive plastic bag will last for weeks of trail walking.

I'd recommend tying your sleeping bag onto the packframe below the bag, and reserving the upper portion of the frame for such heavy gear as stove, cook set, or tent. On many packframe-and-bag combinations, the frame does not extend far enough below the bottom of the bag to allow the sleeping bag to be attached there. In that case, and if you're not carrying a full load, you might consider stowing your sleeping bag in the bottom of the lowest compartment of the pack.

The sleeping bag can be attached to the packframe with shock cords, nylon-web straps, or rope. I've found shock cords the easiest to use and rope the most difficult. A sleeping bag secured with rope almost always slips free, and the knots in the rope will freeze when the rope gets wet.

One last word on packing—or rather, unpacking—a sleeping bag. It's important that you not store your sleeping bag in its stuff sack for long periods when you're not on the trail. When you get home, fluff up the bag (you may also want to let it air in the sun for a few hours) , and then hang it in a closet or store it in an old pillow case. After long periods of compression, the filling—especially if it's down—may lose a good part of its loft. (For more on sleeping bags, see Chapter 4.)

Mattress. A mattress can add a lot of comfort to a camping trip, es-

The bulky, though not necessarily heavy, items need not be packed inside the pack. Such things as a sleeping bag, mattress, and tent can be attached to the packframe and bag.

pecially in cold weather. There are three common types: inflatable air mattress, open-cell foam pad, and closed-cell foam pad.

Although air mattresses provide the most cushioning, good quality air mattresses tend to be heavy and a nuisance to inflate. The thinner ones are liable to tear or be punctured. For that reason, foam pads are more popular. Nothing provides as much thermal insulation as even the thinnest (1/4-inch-thick) closed-cell (Ensolite) pad, although open-cell foam pads are softer to sleep on. Some manufacturers now sell a combination pad, consisting of a layer of Ensolite bonded to a layer of open-cell foam.

When packing, remember that closed-cell foam pads should always be rolled—not folded. If the thin pad is folded and then compressed, it is likely to crack along the fold line. The best way to pack an Ensolite pad is to wrap it around the sleeping bag, and then tie both the bag and the pad as a unit onto the packframe.

Since most open-cell foam pads are too bulky to pack in this way, they are usually rolled as tightly as possible and tied onto the frame next to the sleeping bag. Unlike Ensolite, an open-cell pad may pick up some water in the rain, so, if possible, tie it to the frame beneath the sleeping bag. Some open-cell foam pads are now available in waterproof, nylon cases.

Tent. Except in the roughest weather—or when the insects are so bad that sleeping in a tent is the only way to sleep at all—I leave my tent at home. The reason is obvious: the weight of the tent. Leaving it and the tent pegs behind means saving anywhere from 4 to 10 pounds.

I've found that under most camping conditions, a simple fly—or no shelter at all—will do fine. When properly set up, a fly can be almost as dry as the most expensive tent. In the summer, when the insects are a problem, a "tent" made of mosquito netting provides good protection and weighs almost nothing. The combination of mosquito netting plus an optional fly for wet weather can't be beat.

But if you must take a tent, I'd recommend packing it by tying the tent (preferably with shock cords) as high on the frame and as close to your center of balance as possible. Many packframes are contoured, bending in slightly at the top. That's the place to attach the tent. Tent poles—but not the tent—can be strapped along one side of the packframe. If you use a ground sheet to protect the floor of your tent from wear, it can be wrapped around the tent just as the closed-cell pad is wrapped around the sleeping bag.

Within Easy Reach

There are any number of items—bandanna, camera, canteen, compass, first-aid box, flashlight, knife, maps, poncho, snack foods, and toilet paper—that you may need to get at within a moment's notice. That's where outside pockets are important. With six good-size pockets on your pack bag, you can keep most, if not all, of these items within easy reach. It's not important which pocket you use—as long as you always return things to the same one.

Bandanna. A bandanna is a handy item to wipe your brow, brush away mosquitoes, grab a hot pot off the stove, give yourself a scrub-

If you've got outside pockets, you should use them for those items you may want to reach at a moment's notice. Included in these pockets are such things as a bandanna, camera, canteen, compass, flashlight, first-aid kit, maps, poncho, snack foods, and toilet paper.

down, or wave hello to a low-flying airplane. Tied to the top of your packframe, it's easy to find, and the sun will keep it dry.

Camera. If you take a camera with you on the trail, don't make the mistake of carrying it around your neck. Except for the shortest periods of trail walking, a swinging camera, bumping your chest with each step, will soon become annoying. Camera harnesses have been developed to solve that problem although some people dislike the feeling of being "tied into" their pack by a harness contraption of straps, bands, and cables. If your camera is too heavy or too large to be carried on your belt, consider leaving it at home. If you choose to take it, I suggest that it be snuggled deep into the folded sweater under your poncho and taken out only as needed. There, near the top of your pack, it will be cushioned from bumps, safe from rain, and unlikely to intrude too often upon the pleasure of "just walking."

Canteen. I use a plastic water bottle—rather than the more conventional, saucer-shaped Boy Scout canteen—because I've found that it fits neatly into the upper-right pocket of my pack. It can be brought to hand without my breaking stride. In hot weather, it's a good idea to freeze water or fruit drink in your plastic canteen (with the cap off) the night before you set out. You'll have a refreshing drink with you for most of the next day.

Compass. For hiking on marked trails, the compass almost never comes out of the pack. For finding your way back onto a marked trail, it's invaluable (see Chapter 11). Any outside pocket will do.

First-Aid Box. A first-aid box should be just that—a box, not a "kit." The kits that are commercially available, no matter how complete, are sure to include items you don't want and exclude items you can't do without. I carry a sturdy cardboard box about 6×4×3 inches. In it, I put medical gear, plus an assortment of small odds and ends: sterile gauze pads; Band-Aids; a bottle of Merthiolate; a spare flashlight bulb wrapped in tissue; a miniature pair of scissors; two sheets of moleskin; a small tube of antiseptic ointment; laxative tablets; cold tablets (antihistamine); water-purification tablets; about 6 feet of sewing thread wrapped around a small piece of cardboard, in which I keep my needle; something for an upset stomach; a toothbrush; an oral thermometer; and a snake-bite kit.

In the pocket with my first-aid box—the lower center—I also keep a small assortment of pills in individual plastic (airtight) 35mm film cans. The cans are held together with a rubber band. I label each can: aspirin; antibiotic tablets (for use when a physician is distant); multiple vitamins; salt tablets; pain killer (for emergencies—codeine is one good possibility); and throat lozenges. A little bit of cotton batting or some toilet tissue will keep the pills from rattling.

Despite the fact that most of these first-aid items never leave the pack, I usually carry them all. The added weight is not significant, and there have been many times when I've shared the contents of my first-aid box with other hikers on the trail.

Flashlight. My flashlight (and a spare set of batteries, taped together so they won't get lost) is kept in the upper-left pocket of my bag. Many people use a miniature flashlight powered by AA cells. I prefer a somewhat larger C-cell model because I've found that the little light, while easy to carry, will invariably give out when it's needed most—when finding your way back to camp after dark. Another disadvantage of the little flashlight is that the switch can easily get pushed into the "On" position as the pack jiggles on your back. If you carry this model, place a piece of tape over the switch, or reverse the direction of one of the batteries. The most common problem that comes up with large, D-cell flashlights, aside from their weight, is that the batteries rattle. Try inserting a cardboard tube—such as the one from a roll of toilet paper—into the stem. The little tube will often do the trick. Any flashlight heavier than a D-cell model will be just too heavy to take backpacking, especially if you are using alkaline cells.

Knife. Backpackers don't seem able to agree on where to pack a knife—or even on what kind of knife is best for the trail. Some carry nothing but a miniature pocketknife while others carry those fierce-looking pig stickers. I prefer a folding jackknife with a blade no longer than 3 inches. Such a knife can be used for anything from cleaning your nails to cleaning small game, and will last until it's lost or the blade has been sharpened down to a nub. If you pack a sheath knife on your belt, make sure that the sheath is riveted at close intervals all around the cutting edge or protected by a strip of sheet metal. If it's not, a fall—with the added weight of a backpack on your back—may drive the blade of a sheath knife into your leg. An alternative to carrying the knife on your belt is to secure it high on the frame of your pack. As long as you're near your pack, you're near your knife. And leave your sharpening stone at home. Unless you're planning to be on the trail for a month—or you plan to use your pocketknife for shaving —you won't need it.

Maps. I pack my maps in the accessible, upper-center pocket of my pack. Many packs come with interior map pockets, which are all but worthless for storing maps, unless you stop, put down your pack, and unzip each time you want to know the name of a peak or stream. I keep my maps in a watertight bag. When using loose-leaf guidebooks (the Appalachian Trail Guide series, for example), carry with you only those pages that you'll need and leave the rest at home. Be sure to keep your maps dry; even maps printed on so-called waterproof paper tend to decompose along the fold lines.

Poncho, Sweater, or Windbreaker. It's a good idea to keep rain gear and a sweater close at hand. The obvious solution is to pack these items on top. Most hikers, on the trail during the summer, prefer not to wear rain gear unless the shower is a heavy one. They'd rather strip to hiking shorts and a T-shirt and keep moving. The reason is that sweat builds up fast under any waterproof garment, and the condensation is often more unpleasant than the summer rain. Besides, the poncho, when packed tightly over the contents of the pack, will add extra protection to gear underneath. Just beneath the poncho, I usually keep a sweater or windbreaker. When stopping for a rest or to take in the view, a chill can set in fast as perspiration evaporates.

Snack Foods. Like your canteen, snack foods should be accessible without unharnessing. Whatever your preference—gorp, candy bars, dried fruit—pack it in a double wrapping of airtight plastic or one of those "zip-lock" bags that are especially good for storing items you want to get at frequently. If you leave your pack for any length of time—and when you sack down for the night—seal the bags well and bury them deep in your pack. Hanging your pack from a tree or the beam of the lean-to is often a good idea. Chocolate and peanuts smell just as good to inquisitive animals as they do to you.

Toilet Paper. Two things need to be said about toilet paper: (1) don't forget it; (2) don't get it wet. Small individual sheets wrapped in waterproofed paper and "camper's" toilet paper—rolled without the standard cardboard tube—are unnecessary. To pack toilet paper, compress the roll to crush the cardboard tube and put it in a plastic bag. Tie the bag tightly and remember where you put it. Leaves, even the green ones, tickle.

Additional Tips for Packing Everything Else

Candles. Unless you plan to hit the sack every night at sunset, you'll probably want to take along some candles. Candles seem to last forever, so one or two will be adequate for a long weekend. Candles should be carried in small plastic bags, not to keep them dry but to prevent the inside of the pack's pockets from becoming coated with wax. A lightweight candle lantern does a lot to lengthen the life of a candle and keep the flame from flickering. The cylindrical lantern that I use can be suspended from the roof of my tent with almost no danger of accidental fire.

Can Opener. If you carry canned foods, you'll need a can opener. The GI "hinged" can opener available in camping-goods stores weighs no more than a dime and, once you've had a little practice, you'll find it's easy to use.

Clothes. Clothes that aren't needed while hiking should be buried deep in the pack. They make excellent padding between pots and pans, or between the gasoline stove and your back. One change of underwear, one clean shirt, and two or three extra pairs of socks will usually carry me through a weekend.

Cup. When hiking during the summer, I like to keep my drinking cup where I can reach it every time I pass a clear mountain stream. During the winter, or when good water is scarce, the cup can be tucked inside a cooking pot and taken out when fixing meals or hot drinks. I use a large, plastic cup for camping. I prefer it to the tin cup because the plastic does not get as hot, and to a Sierra-type cup because it holds more and does not spill as easily. If you can't affix your cup to your belt, try suspending it with a loop of cord from the top of your pack. Another good place for it is in an outside pocket that can be reached without unharnessing. Folding metal cups that can be slipped into a pocket are available. The metal cup's disadvantage is that when folded the cup has surprisingly sharp edges, and when unfolded to form the cup, it leaks.

Food. The reason that many backpackers buy prepackaged dehydrated foods is that water is very heavy. Why carry it with you (in the food) when you can add it to the food once you arrive at your campsite? But prepackaged dehydrated foods can be very expensive. There are other lightweight, inexpensive foods in every supermarket that are suitable for the trail. Whatever food you choose to carry, keep it light.

Before you leave home, sort the food you intend to carry by the meal. Wrap each meal individually, and then pack all of the breakfasts together in a larger bag. Do the same for lunch and dinner. This packaging process pays off on the trail. It keeps things neat in your pack and automatically rations your meals. When three days' lunch consists of a loaf of bread and a pound of cheese, the temptation is to eat more the first two days and let the last day take care of itself. When your meals are planned—individually rationed—you're less likely to come home with an empty stomach or with the taste of tree bark and acorns in your mouth. Pack all sweet foods and foods with strong aromas doubly well. If you're packing a pot, store these foods inside it and fasten the lid with a rubber band.

Gloves. If it's cold enough to take gloves, it's cold enough to take mittens. Probably the warmest mittens are down filled, but mittens made of nylon-covered, polyurethane foam are good also. The foam variety is far less expensive than the feathered counterparts. They're as warm as you would like, and they stay warm even when wet. I usually stuff mine into the top compartment of my pack, or under the nylon bands that hold the flap down. Even better is to tie them with nylon cord to the sleeves of your parka.

Hat. In hot, dry climates, a sun hat is indispensable. The best place to pack it is on your head. Make sure that the brim is wide enough in front to shade your entire face, but not so large in the back that it will be knocked off your head by the top of the backpack. For winter hiking (and, especially, for winter sleeping) , try a wool cap. Pack it in the pocket of your parka.

Ice Axe. An ice axe should be packed in such a way that you won't be punctured if you fall. To avoid a serious wound, cover each edge and point with its appropriate safety cap. If your axe didn't come with safety caps, buy some. Many backpacks have loops in the rear of the bag designed to hold an ice axe. Unfortunately, the loops are often down so low that the axe, if secured there, can catch between your legs as you walk. If your bag is built that way, tie a loop of your own higher up on the bag or to the top of the frame.

Ice Creepers, Crampons. Ice creepers are small steel claws that are strapped under the arch of the hiking boot to add traction on snow and ice. They're much less expensive than crampons, which are steel platforms that raise the entire boot some 2 inches above the ground on razor-sharp spikes. Creepers made of molded aluminum do a good job on most slippery hiking trails, and they have the added advantage of not having to be taken off every time the snow disappears. Both ice creepers and crampons should be packed outside the backpack and tied with cord to the top of the packframe. There, they're easy to reach and unlikely to do very much damage to the pack. Protective plastic caps are sold for crampon spikes. Use them; they're designed to protect you, not your crampons.

Match Box. Strike-anywhere wooden matches, safely stored in a match box, make the job of starting a fire a little easier. My match box is made of plastic, which makes a good watertight seal without the need for a special lining material inside the cap. A medicine phial or a plastic 35mm film can may be used also. Pack about half of the matches hot side up and the others hot side down. That way, should you carelessly "set off" the matches in the box while removing one, only half will be lost. This is most likely to happen with metal match boxes. For safety, carry additional matches, wrapped in aluminum foil, in a separate compartment of your pack—and some in your first-aid box as well. I wrap 18 matches in each batch—exactly the number that my match box will hold. When my box is empty, I unwrap a set of 18 matches and insert an instant refill.

Memo Book. If you like to take notes of what you see along the trail, or keep a diary of where you've been, try a pocket-size memo book. Keep it with your maps, or in your shirt pocket.

Pots. Never take more pots than you'll really need. There are any number of delicious one-pot meals a backpacker can easily cook. And some dehydrated meals come packaged in plastic "cooking pouches," which means you have nothing to scrub after dinner. When cooking only for myself, I usually carry a 1½-quart Sigg aluminum pot, with a lid that can double as a frying pan or a platter. To avoid wasting valuable space, I pack the pot full of edibles: gorp, instant coffee in a plastic bag, lemonade mix, etc. Then I pack the pot(s), heavy and full, high and close to the packframe. Don't pack soap pads, suntan oil, or anything else you wouldn't care to eat for dinner in a pot. If you plan to carry "nesting" pots, keep them from banging by filling the in-between spaces with any of the soft items mentioned above and tying down the lids with rubber bands. Frying pans are usually best left in the kitchen.

Rope. A length of rope often proves useful. If you're using a pack-frame that is not of welded construction (that is, a frame made of interlocking metal slats), store your length of rope tightly around the top of the frame. It will add extra strength to the packframe, and the rope is handy for hauling the pack in and out of station wagons.

Saw. If you pack a saw, make sure that it's securely sheathed. "Pocket" chain saws—the kind with rings for your fingers at the ends of a length of abrasive metal wire—sometimes serve in emergencies.

Shoes—An Extra Pair (Or Booties). If you enjoy the comfort of a second pair of shoes to wear while lounging around the campfire, take the very lightest pair you can find. Canvas tennis shoes do very well. I prefer to carry down booties in the winter. They're as light as falling leaves, and they keep my toes warm all night. If you buy (or make) a pair, be sure they have leather—not down-filled—soles. Without leather soles, your camptime wanderings will be limited.

Snowshoes. The best way to carry snowshoes is to tie them with shock cords (not rope) to the back of your pack. Attach them toe up, and weave the cords through the leather webbing to keep the shoes from slipping.

Soap. The easiest soap to pack is liquid soap that is sold in small plastic tubes. One little tube will go a long way. Bar soap is best kept in a plastic soap dish.

Soap Pads. For cleaning messy pots, you'll probably want a soap pad. The soap from these pads can do unpleasant things to the human digestive tract, so wrap them tightly in a plastic bag. Since I don't fry foods on the trail, I leave the pads in the kitchen. For short trips, it's usually sufficient to wipe out the pot with a damp piece of toilet tissue —and then give it a good scrubbing at home.

Stove. If you use a stove for your trail cooking, you probably have one of the small and light backpacker models. Even so, the stove (plus its fuel) is still likely to be one of the heavier pieces of gear in your pack. Pack it high and close to the frame. I like gasoline stoves—the Optimus 8R is my favorite—because the inexpensive fuel is available almost everywhere. Propane stoves, while a little easier to operate, leave you with the problem of disposing of the "empties." Many hikers solve that problem by chucking the used containers under a bush. If you're apt to succumb to this temptation, try a gasoline stove. They're also more fun to use.

Tent Pegs. No matter who you are, no matter how methodical a packer, after finally brushing the leaves off your tent and rolling it into a ball that will fit your tent bag, you'll probably want to gather up your tent pegs (which you've been so careful not to step on) and throw them into one of your pack's pockets. That's what I do practically every time. The problem is that all of the dirt, mud, and caterpillar larvae clinging to the pegs end up in the pack. The tent pegs don't weigh much, but they make a mess. And the sharp ends don't do the pack any good. The best solution is to wrap the pegs in a thick layer of canvas or plastic before stuffing them into the tent bag or the pack. Don't use your plastic ground sheet to do this; the pegs will eat through the thin material in no time flat.

Thermometer. Some people take pleasure in bragging about what they've endured to the folks back home. I once photographed a thermometer to prove that I'd really gone out camping on a day when the temperature fell to 20 below zero. If you're one of these people, you'll want to pack your thermometer where it's exposed to the air but not exposed to breakage. I've never known any backpacker who could keep a glass thermometer for very long. There are plastic models on the market that do a good job, and there are even min-max thermometers that record the lowest and highest temperatures over the course of a hike. They're designed to be mounted to the frame of your backpack.

Water Bottle. If it's necessary to carry more water than you can in your canteens, try a plastic folding water bottle. Water is heavy—a little more than 2 pounds to the quart. Three gallons will weigh 25 pounds. Sitting atop your pack and secured to the frame, those 25 pounds of water will feel about as light as 25 pounds can feel. Wrapped in a damp cloth, they may stay cool. Even if you're not carrying large quantities of water, the water bottle may save many trips to the stream when your shelter is located far from the water.

Some Final Points

Remember that what you leave behind is just as important as what you take. Go down the check list and cross off every item that you can do without *on this particular trip*. Be merciless. Then go down the list again and pare off a few more pieces of gear. The less you carry, the better.

Some fanatical backpackers will saw off the handles of their toothbrushes and snip the labels off their tea bags in a comic effort to save $\frac{1}{4}$ of an ounce. Don't bother. Your time is much better spent thinking what can be left behind. One unneeded pot left in the sink will be worth the weight of 50 broken toothbrush handles.

Always carry a few plastic trash can liners. They have many more uses than you may realize. Of course, they are ideal for storing trash. (Carry out your garbage; there's another hiker behind you.) But they also will make a serviceable, if not durable, raincoat: just cut holes for your arms and head. More importantly, they can make an emergency rain cover for your pack. There's no harm done if *you* get wet on the trail, but if your pack does, you could be in trouble.

Every now and then, vacuum-clean the pockets of your pack. It's the only way to get the trail dirt out of them, and dirt in the pockets means dirt in the gear.

If you want to get the most from your walk in the woods, and you want to camp too, try the hike-camp-hike technique. Hike to a spot you like, set up camp, and then enjoy carefree day hikes without the burden of a backpack. When you've seen the area and you're ready to travel on, pack up your tent, get into harness, and set out for the next campsite. Repeat as often as necessary for a weekend, a week, or a month. It's another way to make your backpacking trip a pleasure and not a plod.

10

On Building a Fire

by Sam and Linda Curtis

Backpacking has many pleasures, but none is greater than those associated with the pungent aroma of wood smoke, the hiss of pitch, and the magic of orange flames. Through the ages, campfires have cast their hypnotic spell on explorers, warriors, voyageurs, and even backpackers. A fire warms the body and the spirit; it adds spice to a hardy meal, light to evening companionship, and moreover it keeps the tigers at a safe distance.

Backpacking stoves, on the other hand, aren't as romantic. Yet they are fast and efficient and convenient. In some areas a stove is the only way to prepare a hot meal because open fires are prohibited. In addition, they don't blacken your cooking pots with soot, and they function well in the rain.

Both cooking fires and lightweight stoves have their places, but their most important function from the standpoint of the backpacker is in the preparation of meals.

The Fireplace

A fireplace is much more than just the specific spot on which your fire rests. As a backpacker, you should be concerned with the materials you use for a fireplace, such as rocks or soil, and you should consider the safety of the general location of your fire and the environmental impact your fire will have on the surrounding area.

For centuries man has been leaving blackened stone rings as proof of his passing. Now, there is nothing magic about using rocks for a fireplace. They don't make a fire hotter or brighter. True, they are convenient for supporting a grate, and they can be arranged so they create an efficient draft, but these advantages can also be achieved with a fireplace that is dug into the ground. A properly constructed fire trench or pit has the added advantage of leaving no indication that you have built a fire there. Just replace the top soil and the sod before you leave, and the area is turned back to its natural appearance.

Recently we took a three-day backpacking trip into a glacial lake in Montana. It was late in the summer season so no one was at the lake, but we must have counted a dozen stone fireplace rings at the most inviting end of the small lake. Four of the fireplaces looked as though they had been built to hold funeral pyres. In addition, all the trees in the area had been stripped of dead wood and even the charred ends of some green saplings poked out of the fireplaces. We'd brought our cook stove, which we used, but any illusion of being in a wilderness was destroyed by those huge piles of stone and the denuded trees.

With the growing number of hikers in the woods, it is increasingly important to pass through the wild areas as unobtrusively as possible. A rock fireplace is pretty obvious, a covered-over fire pit isn't. However, if the stone fireplace is already there *and* there is a good supply of dead wood, you should know how to use the fireplace effectively. In all other cases, learn how to build a trench or pit fireplace, or learn how to operate a cook stove.

A Stone Fireplace. You've come to the end of your all-day hike and the campsite you select has a pile of rocks that has obviously been used as a fireplace. You scout out the surrounding area and discover plenty of usable firewood lying on the ground. So you decide to use the fireplace. How do you use the rocks to your advantage?

There are two things to consider when arranging the fireplace. First, check the air movement. Since a good supply of oxygen is needed for efficient combustion of firewood, the rocks should be arranged in a U-shape with the open side facing the wind. In this manner the incoming air is funneled into the flames and coals to produce a hot fire. The proportions of the rock arrangement is the second concern. Big fires are miserable to cook over because you can't get near enough to them to pick up the pots or stir the goulash. What you need is a small but hot fire that concentrates the heat under the food and not on you. By arranging the rocks so they encompass a space 1 foot wide and 1½ feet long, you create a fireplace that will easily support a small backpacking grill and will also hold a fire that is ideally suited for cooking.

Trench and Pit Fireplaces. If you're going to make your own fireplace, a trench or pit type is the kind to use. They're easy, efficient, and environmentally sensible.

In both cases, any sod and top soil should be removed and placed aside so it can be replaced when you have finished using the area. You should also dig down to mineral soil where there is no chance of decayed vegetation catching fire.

The trench fireplace is long, narrow, and efficient on fuel. The trench should be dug 8 to 10 inches deep, about 2 feet long, and narrow enough to support your cooking pots and pans. (If you have small cooking pots or are camping where the soil is loose and will cave in at the edges, this is not the setup to use.) One end of the trench should be open to the wind and gradually sloped from ground level to the depth of the trench. With this ramplike arrangement wind has a chance to get under the wood. One advantage of a trench fireplace is that it concentrates the heat under your cookware. Also, compared to other fireplaces, it requires only a small amount of wood to produce enough heat for cooking.

The pit fireplace is the alternative for a fireplace that's to be dug in the ground. A 12 x 16-inch rectangle dug down to mineral soil is plenty big enough for cooking. A backpacker's grill will stretch across the narrow side. One of the virtues of this fireplace is that coals can be raked to the front while a regular fire is kept going in the rear.

Fuel

Wood is the universal fuel for campfires. But there are different kinds of wood—dry wood and wet wood, green wood and dead wood, hard wood and soft wood, big wood and little wood. Getting the best wood for a fire is sometimes a matter of choice and other times a matter of finding anything that will burn. There are, however, some general rules that you can follow.

A pit fireplace measuring 12×16 inches is plenty big enough for an efficient cooking fire. This type fire is easy, efficient, and environmentally sound, provided any sod and top soil removed is replaced when you have finished using the area.

Don't cut down living trees to use for firewood—or for anything else. First of all, green wood burns poorly in an open fire. Secondly, the trees around a frequently used campsite have a hard enough time surviving without being hacked up for firewood.

Dry, dead wood is what you want. Unfortunately, dead wood is not always dry. Rain and snow can make the wood-gathering process a real chore. The only thing you can do is hunt for dry wood in protected places—in thick tree and brush cover or under partially fallen trees, for example. Dead limbs and branches on a standing tree are often relatively dry despite heavy rain. However, most popular campsites will be stripped of this source of wood. You may have to roam far afield to get enough dry wood for an evening meal.

If you have a choice, hard wood—hickory, maple, apple, and cherry—will make a better fire than soft wood—pine, fir, spruce, and aspen. Hard wood burns longer and hotter, and makes better coals.

Finally, there's the matter of size. You don't need huge logs to make a good fire. As a matter of fact, wood that's much over 2 inches in diameter makes poor fuel for cooking. The larger pieces take too long to turn into coals, and they need too big a fire to keep them going. Back-

Matches or a small cigarette lighter makes fire starting easy, but tinder is still needed to produce the first flames. Dried pine needles or small twigs are most effective and easiest to find.

packers should be happy with this state of affairs since it means there's little need to carry a saw or an axe. The right-size firewood can be broken into usable lengths with your knee or your foot. If larger pieces of wood are wanted for a warming fire, just put the end of a log in the fire until it has burned or broken off and then feed some more of it onto the coals. There's really no need for cutting it up.

Fire fuel is commonly referred to with words that denote size:

Tinder. This is the smallest of fuels and was originally any highly flammable material that could be ignited with a spark made by striking a flint and steel together. Matches have made fire making much easier, but tinder is still used to produce the first flames in a fire. Natural tinder could be dried grass, pine needles, bark, or twigs. An ideal tinder comes in the form of pine pitch. Pitch is coagulated or crystallized sap and can be found where the bark of a pine tree has been scarred. Pitch burns readily even when wet because, in addition to being highly flammable, it absorbs little if any moisture. We usually carry a 35mm film canister filled with chunks of crystallized pitch for use on those soggy backpacking occasions. A candle stub can also serve as effective tinder. If you let the candle burn under damp twigs, eventually they'll dry out and start to burn.

Kindling. Wood of the finger and thumb size is suitable for kindling. Just as tinder has to be small enough (and flammable enough) to catch fire from the flame of a match, kindling must be small enough to ignite over the heat of burning tinder.

Firewood. If it isn't tinder or kindling, just call it firewood. These pieces may range in size from 1 inch on up to an old-fashioned yule log, but remember the bigger it is the more heat it will need to burn.

Tinder surrounded by kindling in a tepee arrangement burns fast and will produce good coals. The coals can be raked under the grill, giving you a convenient cooking setup.

Laying a Fire

It should be clear that there is a logical progression of fuel size when it comes to laying—or making—a campfire. You start with the tinder, which is the smallest, and gradually increase the wood size. The tinder should be placed in the fireplace and then surrounded by kindling. Still, there are two basic ways of arranging the wood.

A Tepee Fire. This fire lay, if started and maintained in its distinctive tepee shape, is probably the best warming fire. Surround the tinder with kindling so that it forms a cone or tepee shape. As the kindling begins to ignite, add larger pieces of wood to the tepee, being sure not to space them too closely. All fires need air. By keeping the tepee shape as you add wood, the fire will burn with a tall flame thus throwing heat off to people standing around it. The warming effect can be enhanced if you build the fire close to a boulder or rock ledge that will reflect the heat. But don't build the fire directly against the rock as it will leave a large black scar.

A Log Cabin Fire. With this arrangement, the tinder is surrounded by a square of kindling in much the same way that a log cabin is built. The exception is that sticks are also placed across the center of the square to form a grid of kindling for the tinder to ignite. Once this checkerboard of fuel has started to burn, it burns evenly and quickly forms coals for cooking.

Another type fire structure is the log cabin arrangement. The tinder is surrounded by a square of kindling in the same way a log cabin is built. It will burn evenly and quickly produces coals for cooking.

Cooking Over a Fire

If you have never prepared a meal over an open fire, you will soon discover that it requires a bit more know-how than you expected. First, there's the matter of balancing the pots over the fire without dumping the contents into the coals. Then there's the problem of heat control. How do you keep the fire warm enough to cook a meal and cool enough to keep it from burning? What about the sooty pot bottoms?

Let's start at the beginning. After trying everything from a dingle stick—a stick used to dangle pots over a fire—to backpacking grills, we'll take the latter when it comes to the cookfire balancing act. The average backpacking grill measures 5×15 inches, and weighs less than 3 ounces—certainly not too bulky or heavy to carry in your pack. These grills usually have three stainless-steel rods that, when supported on either end, are sturdy enough to hold the largest backpacking pot even when it's filled with refried beans. The trick is to have both ends of the grill well supported. When placed over a trench fire there is little trouble because you've dug the hole in flat ground (haven't you?) and the grill has solid support on each end as long as it extends a couple of inches beyond the trench.

When you are using a stone fireplace, you've got to be more careful. Use the flattest rocks available for holding the grill. If any leveling has to be done, level the rocks so they give even support at both ends of the grill. We once tried wedging pebbles under one corner of a tippy grill; the result was spaghetti dropped on coals.

As for controlling the heat, there are several things you can do. The

With the grill set up in front of the fireplace over coals, any breeze will fan the coals and also fan the flames of the fire. As new coals are formed, they're pushed forward under the grill for renewed heat.

most consistent heat comes from coals, not from dancing orange flames. Those flames are the things that put soot on your pots. To avoid pot black and to maintain some control over your heat, build your log cabin fire at the back of a pit or stone fireplace. As the fire produces coals, use a stick to rake them under the grill. Continue to feed the fire and scoop the coals under the grill until the heat reaches the temperature you want. By piling coals high under one side and low under the other, you can produce a high and low burner. With the grill in the front of the fireplace, any breeze will fan the coals and also fan the flames of the fire and blow smoke away from your cooking area.

Kill the Fire/Bury the Fireplace

At the risk of sounding like Smokey the Bear, *make sure your fire is out—dead out—*before you leave your campsite. Coals, ashes, and any smoldering sticks should be smothered with water. Touch the mess that results with your hands to make sure there's no heat.

When you use a pit or trench fireplace, be sure to replace the top soil and sod carefully. In this way you're not only returning the area to its natural appearance, but you're also making certain that the fire is truly out.

As a last measure before leaving a campsite, we check the area for any tidbits of garbage to be packed out. We also scatter the firewood that may be left. This little ritual is not done with the intention of making other people work for their own wood. We do it because if we're going to go to the trouble of burying signs of our fireplace, it seems stupid to leave the remains of a woodpile to show where the fireplace was.

Stoves

Waiting for coals to get hot, putting fires out, and burying fireplaces takes time, of course. So when it comes to plain efficiency a stove is faster and easier to control. But a stove is more than efficient; sometimes it is a basic necessity, other times it will keep you from going dingdong crazy. There are many areas, Rocky Mountain National Park for example, where campfires are prohibited. In other places campfires are periodically prohibited because of forest fire danger. Some areas are so damp that fires are allowed anywhere, anytime. But starting a fire in such a locale could be the ultimate test of camping skills. And then there are those places where firewood is just hard to find—above the timberline or at a popular campsite. In all of these situations a cook-stove is a necessity. So if you are going to do any amount of serious backpacking, you should have a lightweight stove.

When shopping for a backpacking stove there are many things to consider, but the most basic consideration is the type of fuel it uses.

White Gas. This is the most popular fuel with backpackers. It is easy to buy, it produces a hot flame, and stoves that run on white gas use the same fuel for priming. The fact that stoves using this fuel must be primed in order to vaporize the fuel for burning is seen as a drawback by some people. Also, self-pressurized stoves using white gas must be insulated from the snow and cold for efficient operation. But other fuels have their shortcomings, too.

Kerosene. Although kerosene is the most universally available fuel and it produces a hot flame, stoves using it require priming with a separate fuel—usually alcohol. It is, however, inexpensive and will not ignite easily, as will white gas, when spilled.

Butane. This fuel comes in disposable cartridges. Butane stoves require no priming or pumping. They are like a mini-gas range; just turn them on, light, and you have an instant flame ready for cooking. But butane is relatively expensive, and it is sometimes difficult to find. In addition, it must be kept above freezing in order to operate, thus making it a poor choice for cold-weather use.

Alcohol. Despite the fact that alcohol burners are very light and require no priming or pumping, they have limited use except as emergency stoves. The problem is that alcohol produces relatively little heat and is quite expensive.

What to Look for in a Stove

Weight. Stoves that are suitable for backpacking weigh from a little over 1 pound to close to 4 pounds. That may seem like a limited weight range, but when you start watching the ounces as they add up in your pack 3 pounds can make a big difference. The heavier stoves usually pack more fire power so they're good for family and expedition use or for use in winter when you'll be melting a lot of snow for your water supply.

Compactness. Size and weight don't always go hand in hand. The heaviest stoves aren't necessarily the bulkiest. So when it comes to this feature, some careful comparison is in order. You'll find that some of the smaller stoves will fit inside cooking pots and can be carried in your pack that way. This nesting feature can save a great deal of space.

Stability. A tippy stove is dangerous. It could dump boiling water on you or start a tent on fire. Look for a stove that is designed with a large base and substantial bars or grates for holding pots over the flame. (Although they usually don't come with the price of a stove, make sure you have a pair of pot grippers. They look like a bent pair of pliers and act as a stove's companion piece when it comes to stability.)

Operating Ease. How easy a stove is to operate depends largely upon what fuel it uses. Whether a stove has to be just primed or primed and pumped may make little difference to you considering some of the other features it has. But if ease of operation is the main thing you're after, you'll probably want to go with butane and accept some of its other drawbacks.

Burning Time. Backpacking stoves may burn from 45 minutes to four hours on one filling. Length of burning time depends pretty much on the capacity of the fuel tank, which in turn has to do with the size of the stove. The bigger stoves burn longer. If you plan on cooking multicourse gourmet meals or you have to spend a lot of time melting snow for water, you should look for a stove that isn't going to go out in the middle of meal preparation.

Boiling Time. It may take from 4 to 12 minutes to boil a quart of water at room temperature; the time depends on the stove. The more fire power your stove has, the faster it will boil water. Burning time and boiling time should be considered together when you sit down to figure out whether a stove can get done what you want it to do on one tank of fuel.

Cold-Weather Efficiency. Some folks wouldn't think of camping in the cold. For those who would, certain features already mentioned become especially important. Ideally, a cold-weather stove should have fast-boiling and long-burning times in order to handle the snow-melting chores. It should be relatively easy to operate so you don't have to do a lot of delicate fiddling with hands exposed to the cold. Finally, its operation should not be seriously hindered by low temperatures.

Of course, all this talk of stoves and fires must inevitably lead to a discussion of food.

Food

Food is an incredibly important part of any backpacking trip. Be it an overnight or 8-day expedition, your physical and mental well being will be affected by the meals and snacks you've brought along. Obviously, walking takes energy; an extra speedy pace or heavily laden pack will take even more energy, probably more than you're used to exerting in your everyday routine. Face it, a full 8-hour day of exercise isn't the same thing as your morning pushups. Your body is going to need extra fuel. You can help yourself by planning and cooking well-balanced, nutritious meals and snacks. The trick is finding those foods that will satisfy these nutritional needs, travel well, be easy to prepare, and taste good as well.

We all have our own priorities when it comes to trail foods. Some of us are willing to carry extra weight to ensure gourmet fare; others simply want fast and easy preparation. Your values will shift depending on the circumstances of each trip: will there be a lot of water, will it be hot enough to melt things in your pack, cold enough to freeze them, how long will you be gone, and how much weight can you carry comfortably over a particular kind of terrain?

For a long trip, where weight and compactness are your primary concerns, it is hard to beat prepackaged freeze-dried dinners. There are literally hundreds of them so you're bound to find something that will sustain and nourish you. But be prepared to pay a price; these dinners are expensive.

I've found that you can take some menu ideas from these dinners, then buy the ingredients at your local supermarket, package them for the trail, and be way ahead in taste and finances. Before you head for the store, let's take a look at some of the specifics you'll want to consider when planning your outdoor menus.

Travelability. What makes backpacking food different from garden variety camping fare is that you have to be able to carry it on your back. So unless you hire a team of sherpas, the cooler and ice stays home. Result, limited fresh foods. The same thing goes for lots of heavy cans. A couple of 5-ouncers won't kill you, but this is no place for whole chickens and quart cans of juice.

Another restriction of the backpack is the amount of space available. You won't have room for the dead air space of cartons or boxes. This is where repackaging comes in. Simply empty the contents of the box into a plastic bag. But don't skimp on the quality of the plastic. The rice won't taste very good if you have to hunt for it kernal by kernal in the bottom of your pack.

Plastic tubes and bottles are convenient means of carrying liquids. Honey, peanut butter, jelly, and margarine or cooking oil can all be safely transported in plastic tubes thus doing away with weight or breakage problems.

We have found that spices can transform even the dullest meal into a gourmet delight. There are two ways to conveniently transport your spice shelf. The first is to package the spices for each dish along with its other dry ingredients. For example, if you want to add some onion and parsley to your macaroni and cheese, put it all in one plastic bag. The second method is to use a small medicine vial or film can for each spice you bring along. We prefer this method because it allows some leeway in terms of amounts. You can always *add* a little extra salt to soup, but you sure can't get it out.

Cost. We have already mentioned that freeze-dried backpacking meals cost a lot but may at times be worth the extra expense. When you head for the backpacking supply store beware of purchasing everything you need. Tea, coffee, honey, and cereal will all cost you more than they have to. Use what you have on your shelves at home or buy these staples in bulk. Then bring out the plastic bags, tubes, and bottles and reorganize.

Ease of Preparation and Cleanup. Another important consideration is, how easy will it be to prepare and clean up after these meals? Time is an important factor. After you've been hiking all day you may not want to spend hours preparing your meal. This is one reason why one-pot meals are favorites of backpackers. Starting with a starchy base of noodles or rice, vegetables or meat and spices are added, heated and served all in one pot. To find ingredients that are best suited for this kind of cooking it is important to read directions. You don't want to get caught having to reconstitute dried peas by soaking them for two hours, or being forced to stir a pot of crunchy brown rice for a similarly frustrating length of time. There are all kinds of "instants" on the market that take from 5 to 15 minutes to cook—instant sauce mixes, quick rices, instant potatoes. All can add much to an evening meal over an open fire. Again just be sure to read the labels; what some manufacturers consider "quick" may seem like forever to a tired hiker.

Be sure to check how much water is called for in the directions. If you're scrounging for water in the desert or melting snow, you don't need meals that use a quart of water. This is something to be wary of in dealing with freeze-dried dinners. With some, you have to rehydrate (soak in water) before you ever start to cook. With others, however, you have only to add a cup of boiling water to the contents of a foil pouch and, *voila*, beef stew.

A limited water supply will also affect your dishwashing procedures. When possible, use water that you wouldn't use for drinking; for example, water of questionable purity found in a stagnant pond. Always use biodegradable soap and carry a rough pad for stubborn spots.

Dehydrated foods sometimes require a great deal of water for cooking. Be sure to consider your water supply before heading out on a trip, and pick your campsite carefully.

Never rinse dishes in your water source. I was once filling a canteen from a remote mountain stream only to see someone else's noodles float by.

Gourmet Taste. Variety in both taste and texture is the real key to gourmet backpacking meals. Too often everything tastes the same, like a bland mush. This can be easily remedied by the use of a little imagination and a willingness to carry some spices and an occasional goody (onion, mushroom, green pepper). Remember that this holds true even if you're committed to prepackaged freeze-dried dinners. So why not add something for variety?

The big question is how to vary those one-pot concoctions. Changing textures will really help. Even if you add a different spice every night, noodles will begin to get dull pretty quickly. Try basing your main meal on instant rice or potatoes. Instant rice now comes in a wide variety of grains and flavors—brown rice, long grain and wild rice, chicken flavor and beef flavor.

The next basic ingredient will be some sort of meat or vegetable. There is a wide variety of canned meats on your supermarket shelves, but remember that packing even one small can for each night will add up to an awful lot of weight over an extended trip. We try to balance a few cans with dehydrated soy protein, which can be purchased in bulk in most supermarkets and once cooked, the texture closely resembles that of hamburger.

For a sauce, look to the dehydrated packages. You'll find everything from beef gravy to sour cream, but just remember the warning to read directions.

One trick that will help a mushy texture is the addition of nuts. They are high in protein and unless you cook them to death, they'll remain crunchy. Try adding slivered almonds to your chicken and rice or peanuts to a curry dish.

Mushrooms are another favorite addition. Repackage a small can or bottle in a plastic container that won't leak. Use half on the spaghetti sauce and save the rest for stroganoff. If you like mushrooms, you will most likely head for instant sauces that are labeled "with mushroom flavor." We prefer the real thing, and think the tiny bit of extra weight is worth it.

The same goes for green pepper and onion. As good as dehydrated onions are, nothing beats the crunch of the real thing. It may be too much to carry on a long trip, but what we usually do is compromise— one small onion plus some dehydrated to supplement it.

Some other "additives" may already be in your pack—leftovers from lunch. Real cheese does wonders for a prepackaged macaroni and cheese dinner. And, after a few days on the trail, you may prefer melting it for dinner to carrying it for lunch, especially if the weather is warm and the cheese soft. You may also have some salami or a beef stick that will spice up a bland rice dish.

Spices are really a matter of personal preference and, of course, depend to a certain extent on what meals you're planning. Our staples include salt, pepper, parsley flakes, minced onion, garlic powder, and curry powder. Parmesan cheese is nice to include if you're having spaghetti, and chili powder will put a kick in Spanish rice.

Soups are important to backpacking dinners in several ways. As a first course they quickly ward off hunger pangs and the chills of evening while the chef gets things organized. They also provide extra sustenance for the ravenous eater. Also, the chef can use soups in cooking —tomato, cream of chicken, and cream of mushroom, in particular, all make tasty sauces.

Dessert is something that we seldom indulge in at home and rarely worry about on the trail. A hot drink and a handful of gorp is our usual after-dinner treat. If it's particularly chilly a sweet warm drink will help your body deal with the cold. Try hot Tang or Jello. If your sweet tooth demands a more substantial dessert, we recommend instant puddings or cheesecake. Another special treat is to rehydrate dried fruit in hot water, then add a bit of brown sugar and cinnamon.

The traditional backpacking snack, called gorp, ranges from the basic nuts, raisins, and chocolate to intricate combinations of grains and dried fruits. Our favorite includes dry-roasted mixed nuts, semi-sweet chocolate chips, and raisins. Feel free to experiment with different combinations on your own but do it in the confines of home. On our last trip I tried a cheaper version of our old favorite and it just didn't make it.

Another version of gorp is the gorp bar. It amounts to a combination of the above ingredients baked in a cookie dough and cut into bars. Granola bars are a similar treat—make them yourself or try those found already packaged in your supermarket.

In the long run, of course, you will settle on trail food favorites that will conform to your own idiosyncrasies. Whether you cook on a stove or a fire, you'll get to the point where you can turn out these old standbys with consistent success. Repetition can dull your palate, however. To keep those taste buds alert, it's worth trying at least one new dish on each backpacking trip. We've done that and have come up with some memorable dishes like Hyalite Hash and Cabin Creek Creole. So keep messing around in your *outdoor* kitchen and come up with new tastes of your own.

No matter what your experimental concoctions taste like at home, they'll always taste different in the outdoors. Hopefully the different taste will be more appealing.

11

Using Maps and Compasses

by Jorma Hyypia

A backpacker who has developed map and compass reading skills enjoys a sense of freedom in the wilderness that an uninitiated hiker only
thinks he has. By mastering the techniques of map and compass use,
a backpacker frees himself from a dirt-path leash that often serves as a
tether to personal security. The absence of blaze marks on rocks and
trees will no longer be the cause of incipient panic because he'll know
that although the blazes may be lost, he is not. And when he deliber-
ately strikes off on his own, leaving the wilderness highway to others,
he won't miss the trail guide parade of methodically chronicled landmarks because he'll know how to find his own landmarks.

An experienced map reader may still walk the common trail with
other wilderness travelers most of the time, but he does so as a matter
of choice rather than necessity. When the desire or need arises, he can
confidently leave the trail to seek a distant waterfall or cascade that
trail-bound hikers will never see. He can visit an abandoned mine or
natural rock quarry that other mineral collectors may not even realize
is within easy reach. He may leave the trail to seek a private campsite
in a sheltered location when the trailside shelter, built to accommodate
six people, is already occupied by a score or more of weary, bathless
hikers.

If water supplies run low during a hike through relatively arid coun-

try or along mountain ridges, a good map leads the hiker to water
sources that may not even be indicated on ordinary trail maps. In fact,
advance planning using a topographic map may eliminate the need to
carry excessive amounts of water because there is certain knowledge
about places where water will be available within reasonable walking
distances from the trail.

Backpackers are not the only ones who profit from expert use of map
and compass. A canoeist traveling in lake country saves many paddling
hours by going directly to a portage or connecting stream if he knows
how to lay out and follow a direct across-the-lake route using map and
compass. Such a direct route is especially welcome if the paddling day
turns out to be shorter than anticipated because of bad weather. If you
can use a map and compass, you'll be able to reach the next campsite
a lot quicker than you can by traveling along a more time-consuming
shoreline route.

And if ever another backpacker or canoeist should suffer a serious
accident in the wilds, only an experienced map reader could be relied
upon to take the quickest route, away from marked trails, to find assistance in the shortest possible time. Thus, in the most demanding of
backwoods survival circumstances, map-reading knowledge provides
something far more valuable than the freedom to roam. It provides
freedom from unreasonable fear and panic.

No special expertise is required for the reading and use of many
kinds of maps that are specifically designed to meet outdoor recreation
needs. These include conventional trail maps designed for backpackers,
other trail maps relating to park lands that are issued by federal and
state agencies, and many kinds of special interest maps such as those
that emphasize a state's waterways that are open for use by fishermen
and canoeists. The information contained in all these maps is pre-
sented in such simplified form that anyone can understand it easily
without special training.

Topographic Survey Maps

The limited space available in this chapter is therefore better devoted to an examination of the uniquely informative topographic survey maps prepared by the U.S. Geological Survey. These are available
through many retail and mail-order outlets. To obtain them at the lowest possible cost, order directly from either of two U.S.G.S. distribution
centers. Prices effective in 1976 were as follows: standard topographic

7.5- and 15-minute maps, $1.25; black and white state base maps, $1.50; multicolor and shaded relief county maps, 1:100,000-scale maps, 1:250,000-scale maps, National Park Maps and International Maps of the World, $2 each. For maps of areas east of the Mississippi, including Minnesota, Puerto Rico, and the U.S. Virgin Islands, write to: Branch of Distribution, U.S. Geological Survey, 1200 South Eads Street, Arlington, Virginia 22202. Maps of areas west of the Mississippi, including Alaska, Hawaii, Louisiana, American Samoa and Guam, should be ordered from the Branch of Distribution, U.S. Geological Survey, Federal Center, Denver, Colorado 80225. An index map showing all the topographic maps available for any given state is available at no cost.

If you need topographic maps of sections of your own part of the country, and want them in a hurry or prefer to look before you buy, go to a retail outlet or a library. Check the classified pages of your telephone book for sources. The state indexes provided by the federal distribution centers also list all retailers within the indexed areas that sell topographic maps. There's also a list of libraries where you can consult maps and make photocopies for your own use. However, resort to making copies only if there is no time to obtain original maps. Black and white copies are much harder to read and interpret than are the color-coded originals.

The U.S./Canadian Map Service Bureau Ltd. (a private company not to be confused with any U.S. or Canadian government agency) is a convenient mail-order source of more than 225,000 topographic maps and hydrographic charts. Of course, you will have to pay higher prices to obtain the fast delivery service promised by this company. Two 160-page catalogs, one for each side of the Mississippi River, cost $4.95 each plus 90¢ postage and handling. The mailing address is U.S./Canadian Map Service Bureau Ltd., Midwest Distribution Center, Box 249, Neenah, Wisconsin 54956.

Map makers employed by the U.S. Geological Survey attempt to cram the maximum amount of potentially useful information onto each map without sacrificing intelligibility because of overcrowding with superfluous symbols. What information would be considered useful and what would be deemed superfluous depends on the area of the country being mapped. For example, you would not expect every minor spring to be indicated where the countryside is covered by a network of lakes and streams or other convenient sources of water. On the other hand, even minor water sources are likely to be considered essential information on maps covering desert or open range areas.

Where there are many highly visible landmarks ranging from mountains to large buildings, there is little reason to clutter the map with symbols of fences and small windmills; but fences and windmills might be important orienting landmarks in midwestern areas where there are few if any more prominent natural or man-made features.

Modern topographic maps utilize many colors to convey information quickly and clearly. For example, green is used to indicate wooded areas to delineate them from adjacent areas (colored a pinkish off-white) that have little or no significant vegetation other than grass. Rivers, lakes, and other bodies of water are tinted blue. Red is used for urban areas, and to emphasize important roads, fences, township boundary lines, and the like. When old maps are revised, the revisions are printed in a lavender hue.

About 100 different symbols are used to identify natural and man-made features on topographic maps. As with ordinary road maps used by motorists, various types of lines indicate roads having different surface conditions or relative sizes. Single blue lines represent rivers, streams, canals, and ditches less than 40 feet wide on 7.5-minute quadrangle maps, or less than 80 feet wide on 15-minute maps. Larger streams and rivers are shown to scale, with double lines indicating the two shorelines. Streams or ponds that may contain water only during certain seasons of the year are indicated by broken lines.

Other line patterns indicate footpaths, railroad tracks, fences, and boundary lines between states, counties, parishes, towns and townships, reservations, parks, cemeteries, and other geographic entities. There are special symbols to represent such natural features as sandy areas and sand dunes, marshes, rapids, dry lake beds, scrub forests, and water-inundated areas. Other symbols clearly reveal the locations of such man-made features as buildings, mines and mine dumps, quarries, oil and water tanks, dams, canal locks, orchards, and vineyards.

The most distinctive, and for many map users the most useful, symbol found on topographic maps is the contour line. To the uninitiated, these brown lines seem to wander all over the map in rather aimless ways to form a background pattern having no special meaning. But to a knowledgeable map user these squiggles contain a wealth of information. In a very real sense, these lines add a third dimension to the otherwise flat map. It's the presence of these contour lines that makes a topographic map uniquely useful.

Each individual contour line forms a complete loop, however irregular it may be, even though in some instances it might have to be traced through several adjoining maps to prove that it is indeed a closed loop. Any one line indicates a constant elevation above sea level at any and

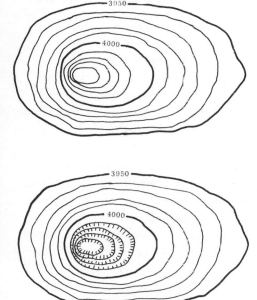

Two mountain tops having virtually identical contour lines can be very different. The top diagram indicates a peak having an elevation of at least 4,040 feet, but less than 4,050. Tick marks on the four inner contour lines of the lower diagram indicated that these contours represent progressively lower elevations. Hence this mountain is about 4,000 feet high and has a crater at least 40 feet deep at the top.

every point along that line. Thus, if you were to walk the full length of any one of these imaginary lines, which exists as a real line only on a map, you would be constantly walking at the same elevation, the one represented by that particular line.

For easier reading, every fourth or fifth contour line is drawn thicker than the intervening lines and has its own elevation marked somewhere along the line. Although on the map the distance between any two adjacent lines may vary considerably, the vertical difference in elevation is always the same on the map in use. The contour interval may be 10, 20, 40, or even 200 feet, depending on what the map maker feels is most convenient for a particular map. The actual contour interval used on a given map is stated at the bottom, but you can easily determine what the interval is just by studying the contour lines themselves. For example, suppose that one heavy contour is marked as 300 feet above sea level, and the next heavy line in one direction is marked 350, while in the other direction the next heavy line is the 250-foot line. You note that there are four thinner contour lines between each pair of dark lines, or five spaces between the adjacent dark lines. Thus each space must represent a 10-foot change in elevation so the contour lines between the 300- and 350-foot elevations must represent elevations of 310, 320, 330, and 340 feet. Going in the other direction from the 300-foot elevation, you would pass through light lines representing elevations of 290, 280, 270, and 260-feet before arriving at the 250-foot heavy line contour.

It is now obvious that just by studying the contour lines you can quickly determine the elevation of any point on the map and also know how much higher or lower it is than some other point. However, you need to apply a little common sense when making such observations about elevations that lie somewhere between two adjacent contour lines.

For example, a point halfway between the 300- and 310-foot contours does not necessarily lie at an elevation of 305 feet on the real landscape because there may be small dips and rises between the contour intervals that could put the point of interest at 302 feet, 304 feet, or some other elevation between 300 and 310 feet. Using a map having a contour interval of only 10 feet the probable error between an intermediate elevation estimated from the map and the actual elevation in the field is likely to be quite small. But if the contour interval is 200 feet, instead of 10 feet, you could expect many more bumps and dips as you climb from, say, the 600-foot elevation to 800 feet, which would be represented by the next contour line.

When you relate the vertical distance between any two contour lines (whether they are adjacent or separated by intervening contour lines) to the horizontal distance between them you derive useful information about the steepness of the slope under consideration. For example, you note that on one side of a hill the 300- and 400-foot contour lines are 1 inch apart on the map; by referring to a graphic scale at the bottom of the map you quickly determine that 1 inch anywhere on the map is equivalent to a horizontal distance (not actual surface distance) of 2,000 feet. Thus you know that in this instance the 100-feet increase in elevation is spread over a horizontal distance of 2,000 feet and that on the average you would have to climb 1 foot for every 20 feet you move ahead horizontally. On another side of the same hill those two contour lines might be only ½ inch apart, which means that to gain 100 feet in elevation you would travel a horizontal distance of only 1,000 feet, or that on the average you would have to climb 1 foot for every 10 feet you move ahead horizontally. Thus the slope on this second side of the hill is twice as steep as on the first side.

On a third side of the hill the contour lines come so close together that the 300- and 400-foot contour lines as well as other lines between them merge into a single line for a short distance. Obviously, this means there is no horizontal distance between the two elevations, and that can happen only where there is a sheer cliff. So watch your step!

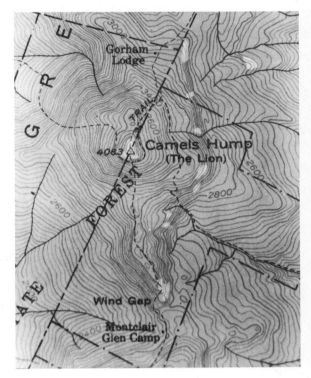

The broken line starting at the bottom center represents a trail leading over the mountain. About midway to the peak the going is easy because the trail crosses few contour lines. Near the peak, the contour lines are packed closely together, indicating the slope must be quite steep.

You can determine the height of a hill, the depth of a valley or canyon, and even the steepness of any slope just by studying the contour lines on a topographic map. By observing the relative spacing between contour lines, you can also anticipate the overall shape of a hill as well as its steepness at any given point. If the contour lines are evenly spaced, the hillside has a fairly uniform slope, allowing for undulations the map is not designed to reveal. If the evenly spaced contour lines are close together, it is a steep and smooth slope; if the evenly spaced contour lines are relatively far apart, the slope is relatively gentle but still basically uniform.

If the contour lines are close together at the top of the hill but become progressively farther apart lower down, expect a slope that is concave in overall shape. If the contour lines are far apart at the top of the hill and progressively closer together at lower elevations, you would expect to find a convex or "bulging" type of hillside.

Brooks and rivers tend to widen gradually in the downstream direction, but a map may show only a short segment of a river and there may be no perceptible change in width. So which way does the stream flow? Contour lines that cross the stream can provide the answer because they form U-shaped loops in the upstream direction. In other words, if the stream runs from the top of the map to the bottom, and the contour lines crossing the stream look like upside-down U's, the water flows toward the bottom of the map.

If you think of a river bed as a long, slanting groove in the ground, and then visualize a mountain ridge as just the opposite—a long and perhaps slanting lump on the ground—you might conclude that contour lines crossing a ridge would behave in just the opposite manner from those that cross a stream. And so they do! Wherever contour lines cross a ridge (and they only cross if the ridge slants) then the lines form U-shaped loops with the bottoms of the U's pointing toward the downhill direction.

To visualize why this should be so, fold a sheet of paper in half, lengthwise, then stand the partly opened paper on a table to form a rectangular mountain ridge. Prop one end up on a book so that it slants from left to right. Now imagine a contour line starting at the left end, a little below the highest point, and running horizontally until it reaches and crosses the fold (ridge). Where does the contour line go then? Clearly, it can only double back on itself on the other side of the paper so that the looped end thus formed points toward the lower elevations of the paper mountain ridge. Turn the paper upside down, to form a slanting river bed, and you can quickly prove to yourself that the contour line U's must loop in the higher, upstream direction. Remember that the contour lines must not parallel the edges of the paper, but must at all times remain perfectly horizontal, or parallel with the table surface.

If you now tie this new information to the things you learned about contour lines as they relate to hills, you begin to realize that the closer together the looped contour lines are packed, the steeper is the ridge line or the bed of the stream, as the case may be. You should also be able to anticipate the profile shape of a ridge depending on whether the contour lines are evenly spaced (indicating an overall uniform slant), or of variable spacing that would indicate either a concave or convex profile.

In very flat country there are no significant elevation changes that could be indicated by contour lines, so you would not expect to find contour loops crossing the streams. In such cases arrows are used to indicate the direction of water flow.

When you move from one contour loop to a smaller loop, it usually means you are going in an uphill direction. But there are exceptions. Let's say that a heavy contour line, marked 4,000 feet, is near the top of a mountain, but your map also shows three smaller loops inside it.

You know that the contour interval on this map is 40 feet, so you assume that the mountain is at least 4,120 feet high but under 4,160 feet.

That would be a reasonable assumption if you were hiking in Vermont, but it could be an erroneous deduction in some place like Hawaii. If the mountain is a volcano, the 4,000-foot contour line might represent the rim of a crater (in which case the mountain is only 4,000 feet high) and the three inner contour loops would then represent successively lower elevations. The bottom of the crater could be somewhere between 3,840 and 3,880 feet above sea level, or from 120 to 160 feet below the rim of the crater.

You can visualize the same kind of problem in nonmountainous areas. For example, in southern cave country you might wonder whether several contour loops represent a bump in the landscape or a depression called a "sink hole." There's a simple answer to the problem. If there are no additional markings on the contour loops, they invariably indicate increases in elevation. If the loops indicate a depression, they will be decorated with short "tick" marks (like coarse fur) that always point downhill. Thus loops indicating a sink hole or crater would have tick marks on the inside of each contour loop. If the small, innermost loop is without tick marks, it means that there is a small bump in the middle of the depression.

What does it mean when a mountain terminates in two separate rather than concentric contour loops? Obviously the mountain has two peaks with a lower "saddle" area between them.

Clearly, an up-to-date topographic map provides a backpacker with just about every conceivable kind of information he wants, thus supplementing the information given in his conventional trail map and guide book. But a word of caution to those who travel by canoe. Although there are symbols for such waterway features as dams, locks, and rapids, a topo map does not usually provide adequate information about water depths, and only the more prominent rapids may be indicated. Thus a canoeist venturing into unfamiliar country should seek additional information prepared especially for the needs of paddlers.

But do not leave those topographic maps behind. They can provide clues to tributary waterways worth exploring, and aid in the location of portages or connecting streams in lake country. They can help you anticipate special canoeing problems by revealing the widths and depths of gorges. And if you are not sure about where you are along a river that has looked very much the same for the past 5 or 10 miles, take a compass bearing on a prominent distant landmark—a mountain, for example—that you can see from the river and that is marked on the topographic map; the information will pinpoint your location along the river.

The borders around the map also contain information that is both useful and often vital to proper use of the map. In the bottom margin area are three graphic scales that indicate map distances in miles, feet, and kilometers. To measure a "crow flight" distance between two points on the map, mark the distance off on the edge of a piece of paper and lay the marked edge along the appropriate scale for comparison. Note that the zero position on each scale is not at the end, and that a portion of each scale is marked off in small increments; for example, on a 1:24,000-scale map the smallest increments are 1/10 of a mile, 1/10 of a kilometer, and 200 feet.

To measure curved distances, as along roads or rivers, lay a length of string or thread along the route to obtain the total length. Then lay the cut string along one of the map scales to determine the total distance. An easier way is to use a map-measuring instrument that can be purchased for a few dollars. It has a calibrated dial with a moving pointer that is geared to a small wheel that is rolled along the route on

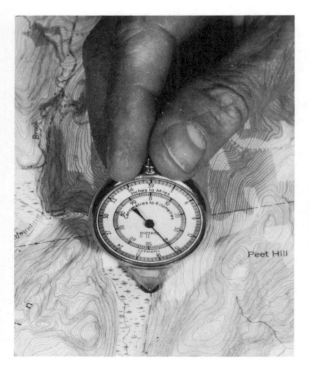

An inexpensive map measurer is a great convenience when measuring distance along curved lines such as roads or rivers. Just set the instrument on zero, run the small wheel along the route and read the measured distance off the dial. If the instrument and map happen to use different scales, reset to zero after noting the dial reading and run to the same position along the distance scale at the bottom of the map.

the map. If the instrument and map happen to have the same scales, read the total distance off the dial. If the scales differ, note where the pointer stops, then return it to zero position and run the wheel along the map scale until the pointer again reaches the observed position. The distance traveled along the map scale is the same as the distance measured on the map.

Near the distance scales is a diagram consisting, usually, of three lines radiating from a common point. The lines indicate the directions of true north (star symbol), magnetic north (MN), and grid north (GN). As shall be seen later, you will make good use of the magnetic and true north lines of this declination diagram. The grid north is of little significance to the average backpacker, so you can safely ignore it.

The name that identifies each particular map is printed in the lower and upper right hand corners; it is commonly the name of a town or some other prominent feature found on the map. The names of eight adjoining maps are marked at the corners and along the sides of each map. Latitude and longitude information to precisely locate each quadrangle is printed at each corner of the map.

To use a map in the field you must orient it so that features marked on the map lie in the same directions as the real features they represent. Sometimes map orientation can be done by simple "inspection," which consists of comparing map and landscape features by eye and rotating the map until they lie in the same directions.

But many times such simple orientation is impossible, for example in deep woods or on open plains where no recognizable landmarks can be seen. The only recourse is to orient the map by using a compass and the declination diagram printed at the bottom of the map.

Usually, true north is made to parallel the side margins of the map and—usually but not always—the magnetic north deviates to either the right or left of true north. To use this information knowledgeably, you should understand why, in most parts of the world, true north and magnetic north do not lie in the same direction.

As you probably know, the earth's magnetic north pole, which seems to "attract" a compass needle, does not coincide with the true north pole, which is one end of the planet's rotational axis. Roughly speaking, the magnetic pole lies about halfway between the true north pole and Hudson's Bay. In the United States, the magnetic and true north poles appear to coincide (just as telephone poles along a straight street can seemingly be made to merge by sighting along the curb) when compass and north star directions are compared anywhere along a so-

called *agonic* (zero variation) line running from the eastern coast of Florida through the Great Lakes.

But everywhere else in the United States it's a different story. To vary amounts, depending on the actual locations, magnetic north appears to be west of true north when a compass reading is taken anywhere east of the agonic line; and the declination can be as much as 25 degrees east at locations west of the agonic line. If you have difficulty visualizing all this, draw lines from various parts of the United States so that they pass through the magnetic north pole indicated on a globe atlas. But bear in mind that any actual *iso*gonic line, which is made up of an infinite number of locations having the same declination, is rarely if ever close to a straight line; most isogonic lines curve noticeably and there are all sorts of localized squiggles caused by such regional factors as natural deposits of magnetic iron ore.

Clearly, to make intelligent use of map and compass you need to know the magnitude and direction of the magnetic declination in your hiking area. The declination is marked at the bottom of the map for the area, but because the declination can change over a period of years, you should verify the information provided by an old map. Do this by locating true north with the aid of Polaris (the North Star) and observing how much your compass needle points either east or west of this true north. Incidentally, it should be obvious that the magnetic north arrow that is printed on the dial of a dime store variety of compass should be ignored because it will almost always be wrong.

Now let's see how a compass is used to orient a map so that the map's true north lies in the same direction as the actual geographic true north. But first this reminder: be certain that no metallic objects are close enough to the compass to affect the needle; move well away from automobiles, and be aware that the head of an axe and even the clip on a ball point pen lying on the map, near the compass, can cause erroneous compass readings. However, don't worry about your aluminum canoe because this nonferrous metal has no effect on the compass.

Lensatic Compass

Two basic types of compasses, each available in several design variations, are sold by backpacking outfitters. Although the traditional lensatic type is clearly the second choice with perhaps the majority of knowledgeable backpackers, a brief description of the way it is used to orient a map is not amiss since some readers may already own such compasses.

A lensatic compass features a floating dial on which degree markings and the cardinal compass points are marked; an arrow indicating north, on the dial itself, takes the place of the compass needle found on other types of instruments. The compass cover flips up to vertical position so that the user can sight at a distant object (mountain, house, tree, etc.) through a slot in the cover that is fitted with a sighting hair wire. There's also a flip-up arm fitted with a small lens that enables the user to see the dial while the compass is held at eye level for sighting.

To use a lensatic compass for orienting a map, place the map on a flat and level surface and open the compass cover fully so that it lies flat (**not** vertically) in the same plane as the compass body. Place the compass on the map so that the horizontal hair wire is directly over and in perfect alignment with the magnetic north line on the declination diagram at the bottom of the map. Now rotate the map, taking

Left

To orient a map using a lensatic compass, lay the sighting wire in the cover over the magnetic north (MN) line of the declination diagram in the map margin. Then rotate the map and compass together until the north-indicating arrow on the compass dial points toward the sighting wire.

To obtain a compass bearing using a lensatic compass, sight through a slot in the compass cover and, at the same time, read degree markings on the compass dial with the aid of a lens at the end of a small arm that flips up to an angular position on the eye side of the compass. To use this type of compass you need to remember actual degree readings.

care not to change the map-compass relationship, until the compass dial swings around so that the north-indicating arrow points directly toward the hair wire. The map is now oriented properly. To double check, turn the compass so that the hair wire lies over and is in alignment with the true north arrow; the north-indicating arrow on the dial should now point in the direction of magnetic north as indicated by the declination diagram.

Orienteering Compass

A newer type of compass, the orienteering compass, is far more convenient for the average backpacker's needs than is the lensatic compass.

A young hiker shows how an orienteering compass is used to obtain bearings. Sighting with this type compass is much easier than with a lensatic compass, and there usually is no need to read or remember actual degree bearings.

Orienteering compasses come in a variety of designs, but a compass of this general type is readily recognizable by the transparent plastic base on which the compass is mounted. The compass itself consists of a rotatable housing with its periphery marked in degrees and cardinal compass points. There's also a large arrow, commonly bright yellow, that points to N, and a series of parallel lines that facilitate alignment of the compass with markings on a map. Note that the yellow arrow, parallel lines, and degree markings all turn along with the housing itself. Also inside the housing, but independently mounted on a pivot, is a swinging magnetic needle that points to magnetic north.

On the base plate, underneath a clear section of the rotatable housing, you will see an important index line, which is the tail end of a long arrow with its arrowhead on the extended section of the base plate. Note that the arrow points away from the compass. The base plate also has various scales that are handy for making distance measurements on a map, and sometimes a plastic lens that can be used to read fine print on a map or to remove slivers from a finger.

Better quality orienteering compasses have a number of extra convenience features such as declination compensation devices and luminous dots and other markings that make the compass easier to use in the dark.

Orienting a map with this type of compass is very easy. First turn the housing so that the north end of the yellow arrow is directly over the index line on the base plate (so that the yellow arrow and the "direction" arrow on the base plate point in the same direction). Place the compass on the map so that either the base plate arrow or one of the long sides of the base plate coincides with the magnetic north line on the declination diagram of the map. Be sure that both compass arrows are pointing in toward the body of the map, not away from it. Without disturbing this map-compass relationship, twist the map so that the red end of the compass needle points to N on the dial. The map is now oriented.

There may be times when you will want to preset the compass itself for the appropriate declination indicated on a map. If it is a west declination (assume it is 10 degrees), turn the compass housing counterclockwise until the index line on the base shows 10 degrees. If the compass dial is calibrated in 5-degree intervals, the index line should be at the second tick mark to the right of north. If the declination is 10 degrees east, turn the housing clockwise so that the index mark is two units to the left of north, or at the 350-degree mark. To orient a map after the declination has been preset in this manner, align one long edge of the base plate with the true north indicated on the map and then swing both map and compass until the needle points to N and lies directly over the yellow arrow in the housing.

Now that the map is oriented, how do you go about finding your way to a distant objective that you may not even see from your present position? If the map indicates that you can probably follow a direct route to the objective, without the need to circle around swamps or other obstructions, you take a bearing on the objective in the following manner. Place the compass on the properly oriented map so that one long edge of the base plate touches both your present position and your objective. Be sure that the direction arrow on the compass base plate points in the direction you want to go.

Now hold the base plate against the map so that it cannot slip, and carefully rotate the compass housing until the north marking is directly under the red end of the compass needle. The needle should be in perfect alignment with the yellow arrow in the housing. The compass is now set for use.

Stand up and hold the compass in front of you at about chest height with the compass direction pointing away from your body. Be sure that you do not have a ferrous metal belt buckle or something metallic in your pocket since such an object could affect the compass needle. Move

When a map is oriented properly the arrow on the base plate (just above the lens), the dial N, and the wide yellow arrow pointing to N all point to true north (which is indicated with a star on the declination diagram). At the same time, the red end of the compass needle points to magnetic north.

your feet so as to turn your entire body until the compass needle again points to north and is over the yellow arrow. The direction arrow on the base plate now tells in which direction you should walk. Pick out a landmark in the near distance that you know can be reached without difficulty even if you have to make some minor detours from a straight path. When you reach that first objective, use the compass in the same manner to line up a second intermediate object. Continue this simple procedure until you arrive at your final destination. Just be sure that as you handle the compass you do not accidentally turn the housing from its preset position.

If you wish to return to your starting point along the same route, hold the compass in the usual way, with the direction arrow pointing away from your body. Next, turn your body so that the red end of the needle swings to the S mark on the dial. Then rotate the housing 180 degrees so that the needle once again points to N. You are now prepared to make the return trip in the same manner, by locking in on a series of intermediate objectives with the aid of the direction arrow on the base plate.

Now let's consider a somewhat different kind of problem. Assume that you are canoeing on a river, or perhaps following a footpath along one shore. The river and its surroundings have looked pretty much the same for many miles and you are not certain just how far you have traveled. But in the distance you see a familiar landmark, perhaps a mountain, that you can locate on your topographic map. All you need to do is take one bearing off that landmark to pinpoint your position.

Orient the map using the compass. Now point the direction arrow on the compass base toward the landmark and rotate the housing so that the red end of the needle points to N. Lay the compass on the map so that one long edge of the base plate touches the landmark on the map, then swivel the entire compass (*not* the housing) until the red arrow again points to N. Check to see that the edge of the base plate still touches the landmark. Your location is where that same base plate edge touches the river. The long reference feature at your location could just as easily be a road or the shore of a lake.

If you are away from all such handy reference features, perhaps in the middle of a forest or in the open plains, you need at least two recognizable landmarks to find your location. Orient the map as usual. Take a bearing on one landmark in the same manner as before, by pointing the direction arrow at the landmark and rotating the housing until the needle points to north. When you apply the compass to the map, you can draw a line that extends in the direction of your location from the landmark. But since it does not intersect a known feature, such as a river, you don't yet know just where along that line you are located.

This is why you apply exactly the same procedure to obtain a bearing on the second identifiable landmark. When you transpose this direction to the map, your position is at the point where the two bearing lines intersect. If a third landmark is visible, use it to check the accuracy of your first two readings.

If you should lose your map, you can still use the orienteering compass to find your way cross country to any landmark that is visible from your starting location. Just aim the direction arrow on the compass base plate at the objective and set the housing N position to coincide with the red end of the needle. Then work your way from one intermediate objective to the next until you reach the final objective.

Note that in none of these applications of compass and map do you have to read or remember actual compass bearings in degrees. This is the main reason why an orienteering compass has it all over the old-fashioned lensatic type.

There is much more that can be learned about the use of map and compass that cannot be covered in a single chapter in a book of this kind. Some of the best information is contained in books dealing with orienteering that you can undoubtedly find at your camping and backpacking outlet. Start your self-training with a topographic map that shows your hometown area. The experience will surely convince you that topographic maps should go with you on that next backpacking trip, wherever it may be.

12

All-Weather Hiking

by Sam Curtis

When I was a kid growing up in rural Connecticut there was only one season for hiking and that was the mild season. In that particular part of the country the mild season was summer and fall when it wasn't raining. During other times of the year, when you could expect rain, snow, or cold, hiking was too much of a hassle to be worth the effort. Equipment was my main problem. I had an old army surplus pack with a primitive frame which, when loaded with even minimum camping equipment, was a bear to carry. To add a canvas pup tent to the pack, along with some cold-weather clothing or heavy rain gear, made the task of carrying the thing pure torture. Consequently, hiking was confined to those months when the weather was mild and there was little chance of more than an occasional shower.

The advent of seasonal hiking came with the improvement in backpacking equipment. The contoured aluminum packframe made the biggest difference. With such a frame heavier loads could be carried with less effort. At the same time lighter materials like nylon were replacing heavy canvas in the manufacture of tents and packs. By being able to comfortably carry heavier loads of lighter gear, backpackers suddenly found that changing seasons didn't have to put a stop to hiking. All seasons were open, although each one posed its own problems.

Basically, hiking seasons are determined by the weather. To talk

Mountainous areas can be particularly troublesome during any season. Wind and air current cause the weather conditions to change radically and quickly. If you're planning on hiking in such a region, be sure you're prepared for all kinds of temperature and precipitation changes, no matter what the forecast.

about spring hiking makes no sense since spring in the canyons of Utah is an entirely different season than spring in the mountains of Montana. Instead it is more logical to talk about seasons as being mild, rainy, hot, or cold. These seasons change with specific locations at particular times of year. As a hiker it's important to know what seasons to expect in order to plan your equipment, but sometimes predicting the seasons isn't easy. I've hiked in the Rocky Mountains when it was the mild season one day and the cold season the next. At times like these, when there is no clear distinction between two seasons, you've got to be geared up for both. Consequently, you have to be familiar with the area in which you plan to hike so that you can be prepared for the extremes you might encounter. Handy sources for this kind of weather information are booklets—issued for every state—entitled "Climatic Survey of the United States." These booklets have monthly surveys of precipitation, snowfall, and temperature from every weather station in a given state. They can be purchased from The National Climatic Center, Federal Building, Asheville, North Carolina 28801.

The Mild Season

When considering seasonal hiking, the mild season is a logical place to start. Until recently, as I've mentioned, mild weather was the *only* time to hike. Consequently, most people just breaking into backpacking still confine their hikes to balmy days and frostless nights. In addition, the hiking equipment and basic know-how needed for this season are common to all other seasons.

The nice thing about the mild season is that it requires no specialized kind of gear or clothing. For a day hike you could probably have a completely enjoyable time wearing casual clothes and comfortable shoes and carrying your lunch in a brown paper bag. At some point you may decide to buy an inexpensive day pack to carry your lunch, camera, and sweater. Eventually, you break down and purchase a pair of boots specially designed for hiking. Most people don't suddenly decide to become backpackers and then go out and buy all the gear and clothing they'd ever need for any season. They accumulate equipment over a period of time as the need arises.

There is no formula for selecting mild-weather hiking gear, but there is a logical progression that seems to be compatible with common sense. Here's the way I'd place them in order of importance.

Day Pack.   Let's face it, if you go for more than one or two hikes during nice weather, that brown paper bag begins to be a pain in the neck. A light day pack is much more convenient for carrying some food and extra clothing. And, who knows, you may just need that extra clothing.

Hiking Boots.   For a while such things as sneakers and work shoes will do fine. For years I wore a pair of army boots as my hiking boots. But when you start to reach the outer limits of day hiking—those 8- to 12-mile circle trips—your feet are going to ache for something that offers more support and cushioning. A good pair of hiking boots is relatively inexpensive but will last for years if given proper care. One mistake many people make is to go out and buy a pair of heavy boots when a medium or even light pair could have met their needs. When you get into rocky terrain where you'll be crossing talus slopes and snow fields, heavy boots are useful. For most hiking situations, however, mediumweight boots are best.

Frame Pack.   When day hikes seem to be too short and you get the urge to start taking overnight trips, you're ready for a packframe and bag. This is the item that has changed the nature of backpacking and will allow you to carry, with relative comfort, all the things you need to be self-sufficient for days at a time.

Sleeping Bag.   You might try packing a blanket roll in your new pack but it won't be long before you'll want to invest in a sleeping bag. There are numerous weights, designs, and materials available. For the mild season, a light to medium bag will serve well.

Stove.   A backpacking stove is more than a convenience these days. In many areas wood fires are prohibited. Even where fires aren't banned, stoves are often desirable for both ecological and aesthetic reasons. There are a wide variety of lightweight stoves available, all of which function well in mild weather.

Tent.   A tent isn't a must during the mild season. You can string up a plastic or coated nylon tarp if you want to keep the dew off and the starlight out of your eyes. A tarp will even keep you dry—if pitched properly—during a summer shower or thunderstorm. It really isn't until you arise, after a sleepless night, with your eyes swollen shut by bug bites that you'll consider laying out the cash for a tent with built-in mosquito netting.

Clothing.   Clothing during the mild season is not much of a problem. You should be able to get along with what you already have hanging in your closet. Perhaps the one exception is a coated nylon poncho that is light, inexpensive, and practical for warding off an unexpected 15-minute shower.

When selecting your hiking clothes avoid garments that might cause chafing. These include clothes that are tight, rough, or stiff. Sleeveless shirts and halter tops don't work well either because they have a way of getting under your pack's shoulder straps or back bands, places where you're particularly susceptible to rubbing.

When it comes to hats for sun protection, those wide, stiff brimmed

numbers just won't work. The brim will keep banging into your packframe and you'll lose your hat or your temper—or both. Try a soft
3-inch brim instead. If you don't wear a hat, you risk exposing your
neck—an area that's particularly vulnerable—to sunburn. Glop it up
with sun screen.

Finally, stay away from narrow, braided, or knobby belts. They make
designs in your back after being pushed upon by your pack all day.
A wide thin belt is your best bet.

The Rainy Season

You may be wondering who, with any ounce of sanity, is going to
hike in the rain. The fact is that quite a few folks do, especially those
who want to get away from the fair-weather crowds.

The main concern during the rainy season is keeping dry. However,
there is the school of thought that supports the fatalistic approach—if
it rains you *will* get wet. Hikers of this persuasion don't bother with
rain gear—except at night when they shake off and climb into a dry
tent. I'm of the school that says you should try to stay dry, but if you
can't, don't be too surprised.

At the root of trying to keep dry is the water repellent vs. waterproof
controversy. Simply stated—are you going to get less wet using water
repellent or water*proof* rain gear? Water repellent materials will shed
rain for a while. In a light drizzle you might hike for hours before
noticing the slow seep of moisture. You'll probably be wet in five minutes if you get caught in a real downpour. But water repellent materials breathe—they are porous enough to let body moisture out at the
same time they are letting some rain come in.

Waterproof materials, on the other hand, don't let rain in and also
don't let perspiration out. So you are protected from outside moisture
while inside you stew in your own juice. The solution to the problem
is largely a matter of taste, but here are the leading possibilities:

Rain Suit. These waterproof outfits range from cheap, light plastic
suits to expensive, heavy, rubberized ones. If the rainy season you plan
to walk through comes with real gully washers, it's worth carrying one
of these suits. I'd choose a lightweight model. I'd also try to get rain
chaps instead of rain pants. The chaps cover neither your rear end nor
your front end, so there is some breathing room.

While backpacking in a rain suit may be like sitting in a steam cabinet, the garment should be included in your gear. The suit is extremely handy for in-camp use during the wet seasons of spring and fall.

Cagoule.   This is an ankle-length waterproof pullover that resembles an old-fashioned nightshirt with a hood. Both the hood and the shirt bottom have drawstrings so you can really seal in the sweat. Cagoules are good for around the camp use, but I find them a bit too confining and hot on the trail.

Poncho.   Many people are familiar with the heavy, rubberized army surplus type of poncho, the 4×7 foot rectangles with a head hole and a hood in the middle. Those versions have served many hikers over the years. But light nylon ponchos have replaced the heavy army ones. They are highly water repellent and have some breathability but can still make you drip inside if you wrap yourself up too tightly. Of course the virtue of the poncho is that it can be worn fairly loosely, giving you adequate rain protection while wafting away most of the unwanted body heat at the same time. A good backpacking poncho is longer in

No matter when you're backpacking, never underestimate the value of a good tarp. The coated nylon tarps, when pitched properly, can withstand an amazing amount of wetness. If you do a lot of hiking in rainy seasons or areas, you should consider taking along a tent.

the back than in the front, so the rear flap can go over your pack. If I'm expecting anything less than torrential rains, the poncho is my choice in wet wear; it has the added advantage of doubling as a make-shift shelter.

Footwear.   If you're going to wear regular hiking boots, the only choice is to coat them well with water sealant and take some more sealant with you. Otherwise, under constantly sloppy conditions, you might want a pair of boots with rubber bottoms and leather uppers. They aren't the perfect hiking boots, but they'll keep your feet rela-tively dry.

No matter how wet you get during the day, you're going to want to sleep dry. To do this you have three options: don't take any overnight hikes during the rainy season; use a tarp; use a tent.

Tarp.   Obviously, a tent offers more protection than a tarp, but a tarp shouldn't be underestimated. Coated nylon tarps are light and compact and can withstand an amazing amount of weather.

One fall night in a remote section of Canyonlands National Park I remained dry through a howling succession of rain, sleet, and snow. I didn't sleep much because of the noise, but I was dry when the still, gray morning dawned.

For light rain or drizzle, tarps work fine when pitched in the traditional pup tent manner—an upside down V. For more protection from driving rain, pitch one end of the tarp low against the wind and the other end high enough to sit in. When you're sure you are going to get into heavy rains, you'll have to move up to bigger and heavier things.

Tents.   The ins and outs of tents are discussed in detail in Chapter 5. Here let me mention only the very basic differences. Most backpacking tents made today have a ceiling of breathable nylon over which a waterproof rainfly is placed. The inner ceiling lets condensation and moisture escape from inside the tent while the rainfly, which is separated from this ceiling by several inches, keeps moisture out. There are a few tents, however, that have just one ceiling, which is coated to make it waterproof. These tents pose the same problem as waterproof clothing: they hold in moisture and soak you in your own sweat. So, if you can afford the price, get a tent with a rainfly.

A good shelter should keep you and your gear dry. That is expected. But the rainy season seems to have a way of insinuating its presence into everything—even your sleeping bag. Down sleeping bags are great most of the time. They are light and compact and warm—until they get wet. Then they are relatively useless as an insulator.

One alternative for hikers who'll be spending a lot of time backpacking in the rainy season is a bag filled with a synthetic material. This synthetic filling will provide insulation even when it's wet, it can be wrung out easily and dries quickly. It has more weight and bulk than down, but when you are constantly surrounded by moisture, it's worth having along.

Cooking in the Rain

It's unpleasant. Beyond that it can range from rather frustrating to absolutely infuriating. You can do two things to keep the experience and the food palatable. First, use a tarp or a poncho to make a sheltered kitchen. When a wind is blowing you'll want to pitch the tarp low. But if the rain is coming straight down, tie the tarp high enough so you can stand up. Second, bring a stove to do your cooking. You can build a fire in the rain (see Chapter 10), but a backpacking stove will save you a lot of time and energy.

I wouldn't recommend using your stove in the tent. When you are crowded in there with all your gear, your arms, elbows, and feet have a way of getting in the way. You may get burned or knock over your food or set the whole place on fire. Keep the stove in the kitchen. Keep the kitchen outside.

Wet-Weather Precautions

Hypothermia. Simply stated, hypothermia is the loss of body heat. In its most extreme form it causes an irreversible downward spiral of the body's core temperature and results in death. You are most susceptible to hypothermia when you're tired, wet, and cold because under these conditions your body's heat-producing mechanism is not very efficient. Hikers in the rainy season, particularly when it's chilly, should be alert for the symptoms of hypothermia—uncontrollable shivering, difficulty in speech, loss of manual dexterity, collapse. The shivering usually comes first. At its outset the victim should change or be changed into dry clothing, be protected from wind and rain and fed a hot liquid and high-energy foods. Build a warming fire if you can. Under extreme conditions, put the naked victim in a sleeping bag with someone else who is also stripped. Sometimes this is the only way of warming a person whose own body is unable to generate any heat.

Hypothermia is usually associated with cold weather, but I've seen its shivering stage in July when the temperature was about 50 degrees. Don't ignore its signs during any season (see Chapter 13).

Lightning. If your rainy season happens to coincide with the electrical storm season, you ought to know something about the ways of lightning. It usually will strike the highest point around—a mountain summit or exposed ridge, a tall tree, or a tall person standing on a barren plain. Stay as far away from these places as possible. Get rid of any metal objects that you might have and hunker down on the ground with some insulation, like a sleeping pad, under your feet. Don't lie on the ground. If lightning travels through the earth at the point you happen to be, you'll want as little of you as possible in contact with old terra firma.

Flash Floods.   These are usually associated with arid desert country. But disasters such as the 1976 flooding of the Big Thompson River near Estes Park, Colorado, are potent reminders of the potential for flash floods in unexpected areas. Selecting a safe campsite is the most important consideration. Keep away from dry washes and other natural drainage areas that will collect water. High knolls or plateaus are your best best for a safe camp. When hiking in narrow canyons be aware of the possibility of flooding and be sure you'll have an easy escape route. If you can't get out of a canyon, don't go into it during the rainy season.

The Hot Season

A friend of mine recently brought a small can of chili peppers on a hike. During our lunch break he opened the can and contentedly started popping chilis. When he offered me one, I innocently downed the whole thing. The fire, the tears, the incredible heat just about did me in. My friend was amazed. He swore the peppers weren't *that* hot. I couldn't see and couldn't speak, so I obviously disagreed.

People react to air temperatures in the same way. Your hot season may start at 80 degrees while your buddy's doesn't begin until the temperature hits 100. He enjoys hiking in the desert in August while you swim in sweat backpacking through the same country in May. You are the only one who can say when your hot season begins. So plan your trips and gear with your own body's thermometer in mind.

There are two popular theories when it comes to proper dress for the heat. One says put it on; the other says take it off. Natives of the hot, sandy Arab countries are put-it-on folks. They greet the heat with long flowing robes and engulfing head gear. The idea is that the less sun reaching you the better.

When applying the cover-up principle to backpacking, light-colored long pants, long-sleeved shirt, and hat will do the trick. The light colors help reflect the heat. You'll find that a hat with some sort of ventilation on the crown will keep you from becoming a hot head.

Advocates of the strip-down theory may hike in nothing but socks, boots, underwear, and shorts. Personally, I find that a T-shirt between me and my pack's straps is needed to prevent unpleasant chaffing. Also, a real danger in taking off most of your clothes is sunburn.

Actually, the best way to keep cool is to wear wet clothes. Where plenty of water is available, periodic dunkings will keep your clothes wet and you will be cooled by the process of evaporation. I've used this method often and it is extremely efficient. But when water is scarce, you'll have to stick with putting things on or taking them off.

Much of beating the heat comes in careful planning. In extremely hot weather you won't want to be hiking during the hottest part of the day. Morning and evening hiking will cut down on your mileage, but sometimes it's the only reasonable way to go. By sitting down with a topographical map before your trip, you can attempt to chart a route that will bring you to water, shade, or both, during that hot, siesta time of day. A note of caution, though. In desert country, water sources —even those indicated on maps—can be very unreliable. Check on water conditions with knowledgeable local folks before placing your money on a spring that may be dry.

Shade is often the difference between a tolerable resting place and one that isn't worth the stop. For this reason you might want to carry a light tarp to string up and use as a sun shade when natural shade isn't available.

Cooking. It would be great if you could always plan noncook meals when hiking in the hot season. Unfortunately, weight requirements often necessitate the use of freeze-dried foods. These need cooking, if only in the form of boiling water, so some heat source is required.

I'd stay away from using a fire since it isn't very efficient and spreads a lot of heat on you. A stove and fuel will add more weight to your pack but will make cooking much more pleasant. Avoid taking self-pressurized stoves, however. They tend to generate too much pressure when it is hot and release vaporized fuel through their safety valves. I have a friend who douses his stove with water whenever this happens —which is about every ten minutes—and then relights it again. If you have his kind of patience, fine. Otherwise stay away from pressurized stoves when it's hot.

Water. Your body needs water. It needs more water when it's hot. Unfortunately, the hot season often means arid country where natural water sources are difficult to come by. When you aren't absolutely certain of water sources along your route, you'll have to carry your own supply—enough to get you in *and* out. The average person will need about a half gallon for drinking and eating per day if he uses his water sparingly. Of course, water can be found in arid country. Rain water catches in rock potholes in canyon country. Intermittent streams some-

If you're traveling through a desert region during the summer season, you should be on the lookout for water stains on the walls of canyons. A small pool below the cliff may be the only source of water for miles around.

times have sheltered holes containing water from the last storm. When you do find this kind of water supply and have any question about its purity, boil it for 10 minutes or treat it with purifying tablets.

The most important thing is to have enough water for your return trip. If you haven't found water by the time half of your water supply is gone and there is no guarantee of finding water, then it is time to turn around and head back to your starting point.

Hot-Season Precautions

Sunburn. Sunburn is possible whenever the sun is out, regardless of temperature, but in the hot season, with the use of the take-it-off method of cooling, sunburn problems are more numerous. The surest way to keep from getting sunburned is to stay covered up, either with clothes or a sun block.

Once overexposure to the sun has occurred there is little to do. If you have sunburn cream it may relieve the pain, and aspirin should help the accompanying headache, but an early eye to prevention is the best procedure.

Heat Exhaustion. Heat exhaustion, the most common heat-related illness, is a real possibility if you push too hard during hot weather. You'll feel extremely tired and might have a headache and nausea. Profuse perspiration often occurs. That is Mother Nature's way of cooling you off. The patient should rest and drink a solution of half a teaspoon of salt to half a glass of water every 15 minutes for an hour.

Sweating takes water, salt, and some chemicals from your body. That is why you must drink more liquids during hot weather and that's why it's a good idea to carry salt tablets with you. Taken as recommended on the bottle, these tablets can help prevent heat exhaustion.

The Cold Season

Of all the seasons, none has been opened up more by modern backpacking equipment than the cold season. Camping in the cold used to be left to trappers, a handful of mountain climbers, and the Swiss Army on maneuvers. Now a fast growing number of hikers, cross-country skiers, and snowshoers are going out in the cold and snow and camping in comfort.

Wool, down, and synthetics are really the only materials to consider for cold-weather clothing.

Wool. This material has long been the choice of winter outdoorsmen. Wool worn from head to foot—socks, underwear, pants, shirt, sweater, hat, mittens—along with a nylon windbreaker, has gotten me through four days of mountain snow and cold—five degrees below zero —very comfortably. Wool retains much of its insulative quality even when it's wet. So if you're prone to taking tumbles in the snow, wool can be relied on to give you some warmth. It is, however, relatively heavy and bulky, making it cumbersome to pack. Nevertheless, I still find myself favoring wool for most of my cold-season outings.

Down. Both goose and duck down are ideal, in many ways, for the backpacker. Clothes and sleeping bags filled with down are light, compact, warm, and comfortable. They stay warm until they get wet, and

During colder seasons you'll have much more control over your comfort if you use the layer method of dressing—slipping shirts, sweaters, windbreakers, and parkas on and off as you go along.

that's the hitch. When your cold season is dry or snowy, but with extremely low temperatures, down should be fine in both parkas and sleeping bags.

For clothing it's better to have many layers than to have only one or two. You'll have much more control over your body's temperature if you can put on or take off different layers of clothing. With a turtleneck and a heavy parka, for example, you don't have much control.

When dressing for a winter outing, you must remember how fast conditions change. If you're cross-country skiing or snowshoeing on a cold but sunny day, you can work up a good sweat, but when the sun goes down and you're coasting home or into camp, you'll really need that extra layer you've been carrying. One such afternoon, I returned home to find two friends shivering uncontrollably in their soaking wet blue jeans and cotton shirts. What had started out as a pleasant afternoon of skiing, ended in the first stages of hypothermia.

Tents. A good tent for the cold season will be a good tent for any other season, except it will have a few convenient cold-weather features. When selecting a tent to be used in the cold, particularly in snow, look for snow flaps, frostliner, two entrances, vent hole, cook hole, and roominess.

Pitching a tent in the snow requires a bit more effort than pitching one on the bare ground. To make a stable tent site you have to compact the snow by stomping down the area while wearing your skis or snowshoes. If you keep your pack on while doing this, the snow will compact even better.

When it's time to stake the tent down, the skinny pegs that you used in the summer are useless. You'll need 10- to 12-inch curved aluminum snow pegs to provide adequate surface area to hold in snow. For alternatives to pegs you can use snowshoes, skis, and poles or dead branches. Remember though, if you use your means of transportation for anchoring the tent you'll have to stay close to camp.

The packing and pitching process will take longer in the cold season than making the average summer camp. So you'll want to look for a camp site well before dark. Keep in mind also that dark may set in early in the afternoon in the cold season.

The Winter Kitchen. Except in really foul weather, you'll be able to cook outside. If you don't want to eat early—before dark—you can carry a candle lantern to illuminate your food preparations, which will probably call for water as a major ingredient. Water can be difficult to find in cold weather. Lakes and even streams are often frozen, which means chopping holes. And sometimes there is nothing but snow.

Getting water from snow takes time and burns fuel. When I know snow will be my only water source, I carry twice as much fuel as I normally would. Dry powder snow has the lowest water yield, while old compacted snow has the greatest yield. If you dig down toward the ground, you'll get into that older stuff.

If you're camping in the snow, use a stove. Firewood is difficult to locate and fires built on snow sink slowly away from you. Stoves are much more convenient, but just any stove won't do. Butane stoves don't operate effectively unless the fuel is kept above freezing, so they make a poor cold-season choice. Self-pressurized stoves work in the cold but they need to be protected from the cold ground or snow with a piece of closed cell foam or other such insulation. Probably the best winter stove is one that uses white gas and has a pump to maintain pressure.

Access to a pair of snowshoes can open up a whole new world of backpacking. No matter how deep the snow, you'll be able to get out. Touring skis are another possibility for winter or snowy-weather backpacking.

Getting Around. Part of the adventure of camping in the snow is the getting there. Skis and snowshoes are the devices that allow backpackers to extend their activities through the whole year. Both of these means of over-snow transportation require some practice. You shouldn't try them with a pack on your back without first mastering the fundamental techniques. But once you get the hang of these contraptions, you'll find they open up a new world of hiking enjoyment.

Snowshoes. I'd advise snowshoes for those folks who aren't the most surefooted of animals. They will provide a stable, if somewhat slow, means of snow travel. Snowshoes come in a variety of designs, but for backpacking the long, narrow shapes, usually called the Alaskan or Trail, work best. These offer plenty of surface area for good flotation and their tails drag slightly to keep the shoes on a straight course. Snowshoes of this type that measure 12×60 inches will support up to 200 pounds. A 10×56 size will carry from 150 to 175 pounds. This traditional design is made with a white ash frame and rawhide or neoprene webbing.

There is a relatively new snowshoe on the market that is also suited to backpacking. It is made with an aluminum frame and neoprene webbing. The advantage of this is its light weight.

Cross-Country Skis.   Skis offer the ultimate in winter travel. On the flats, you can glide along faster than you could walk and on the down-hill grades you can really fly. The big thing to remember when select-ing cross-country skis for backpacking is that you'll be carrying extra weight. Light racing skis, and even light touring skis, are not going to give you enough flotation. In flat and hilly country you'll want a gen-eral touring model, and I'd suggest a simple cable binding over the toe clamp binding. In mountain terrain you should go to the wider moun-taineering models that have metal edges along 2 or 3 feet of their bottoms.

Another possibility is the waxless ski. Traditional cross-country skis require the use of different kinds of waxes applied to their bottoms in order to provide both grip and glide. In recent years, however, ski man-ufacturers have come out with skis that don't require wax. One version has a fishscale pattern stamped on the plastic bottoms; another has strips of mohair attached to the bottoms. In both models, you get for-ward glide but no back slip. I've found the fishscale skis produce an annoying whistling sound on downhill runs and the mohair skis have a sluggish forward glide. But if you ski in constantly changing snow conditions, you may find waxless skis preferable to constantly changing waxes. *Note*: Skiing with a pack on your back requires some getting used to, and you'll find that most frame packs are not ideal for ski backpacking. The important thing is to keep the weight in the pack as low as possible. If you can adjust your bag to a lower position, do it.

Cold-Season Precautions

Hypothermia (see Wet-Weather Precautions) .

Frostbite.   Ear, nose, cheeks, hands, and feet are the most vulnerable parts of the body when it comes to frostbite, which will appear as white spots on the skin. By using a buddy system to check for such white spots, you can usually avoid any serious problems. Of course, adequate protection in the form of a wool hat and parka hood should be used. Detecting frostbite in feet and hands is another matter, since you can't see these areas when they are covered with clothing. When-ever feet or hands feel extremely cold or start to ache, it's time to apply extra warmth through exercise, more clothing, a warming fire, or high-energy foods. Cold hands can be placed against the skin of your arm pits or crotch for warming. I've even put a companion's cold feet against my stomach to warm them up. It helped her feet but was rough on my stomach.

In cases of severe frostbite, the only advisable procedure is to get the victim to professional medical help as soon as possible. Don't rub frostbite or try to rewarm it on the trail. Don't let the patient smoke or drink alcohol.

It has been found that rapid and complete rewarming of frostbite in water heated to 108° to 112° F. is the best medicine. But it is important that the victim be in a situation where he can have continuous rest and warmth after the reheating. Half-hearted attempts to reheat severely frostbitten areas on the trail often cause more damage than would result by doing nothing at all.

Avalanche.   Snow slides are the result of many complex factors, some of which are not completely understood. You don't have to be an avalanche expert, however, to avoid their dangers. Don't travel in areas where avalanches are likely to occur. Most avalanches happen on open slopes of 30 to 45 degrees. Old avalanche chutes are often visible in mountainous areas and should be avoided. The safest routes are on ridge tops or in valleys, away from the bottom of slopes. Areas covered with large trees and rocks, or with heavy brush, are usually safe.

If you must cross areas with potential avalanche hazards, cross them near the top of the slope. Let only one person cross at a time while the others watch his exact location. Use an avalanche cord—a long piece of colored nylon cord attached to the body—that will float on top of the snow and indicate your location if you should happen to be caught in an avalanche.

It seems to make sense to talk about avalanches when discussing cold-season hiking, yet I've been worried about them on spring hikes when I was stripped to shorts and a T-shirt and concerned about getting a bad sunburn. It should be emphasized that seasonal hiking is indeed changeable and seasons often overlap. You have to know the weather in the area you plan to hike in order to be prepared for the extremes that may occur in the space of a few days. When you are ready to cope with the seasons, you'll be free to enjoy the varied pleasures that have brought you into the weather—even if it does get hot, or cold, or rainy.

13

Safety and First Aid

by Dave Engerbretson

To some, backpacking is a never ending succession of glorious sunsets, deep blue mountain lakes surrounded by lofty peaks, and pleasant companionship in idyllic settings. To others, it is a sport fraught with danger, hard physical labor, stinging bugs, lurking snakes, and growling bears. In truth, reality lies somewhere between these two extremes. But the danger, hard work, and discomfort are occasionally as real as the pleasures, and the backpacker must be prepared to cope with these situations if the ultimate rewards are to be achieved. Fortunately, with a little forethought, even the beginner can embark on his first trip confident that he is well equipped and capable of meeting almost any problem that may confront him. Without this planning, though, the poorly prepared novice may have such a miserable experience that he will give up the sport in disgust.

To ensure a successful initial experience, a trip should be planned that is well within the capabilities of every member of the group. This should not be a major expedition, but, rather, a simple hike over well-established trails close to civilization.

With experience, trips can be more demanding, but the first few should be considered merely "shakedowns" of yourself and your equipment. If possible, try to find an experienced backpacker to accompany you. You'll learn more in a single outing with an experienced friend than in many trips with a group of beginners. Be certain, too, that you have spent some time in a physical conditioning program to prepare your body for the rigors of the trail (see Chapter 7).

When packing for a trip, give careful consideration to all weather conditions that are likely to be encountered, and make certain that you have appropriate clothing to meet every possibility. The safest rule is to count on bad weather, and go prepared for the worst. If you have good weather, great. But if you have foul weather, you'll be able to handle it.

There are a few items of equipment that should be carried on every hike whether a day trip or one of several weeks. In fact, these items are especially important on a day hike, since they will enable you to meet a variety of emergencies, including an unplanned night in the woods. Many serious and even fatal situations have resulted from hikers failing to carry one or more of these items on "just a short hike."

Your pack should always contain the following: extra food (light weight, high calorie), extra clothing (at least a sweater and combination wind/rain jacket), map of the area, compass, knife, small flashlight, light nylon cord, candle (for starting fires in wet weather), matches in a waterproof container, first-aid kit, and a large plastic drop cloth or, even better, a Space Blanket. In addition, such things as water, sunglasses, insect repellent, snake-bite kit, personal medicines, and so on should be carried where appropriate.

Before leaving home, a brief itinerary of your trip should be left with friends, relatives, and/or a forest ranger near where you will be hiking. In the rare event that you get lost, are delayed by an accident, or someone needs to reach you, the itinerary will save a great deal of time and effort in locating you.

Backpacking alone in the wilderness can be a very satisfying experience—if everything goes well. From a safety standpoint, however, there is little to recommend the practice, and it should be avoided until the hiker has gained extensive experience. Even then, considerable risk is involved. For safety, three is the minimum number that should attempt a serious backpacking trip in true wilderness, and four is even better. If one of the group is injured, one can stay with the victim, while two go for help. A sick or injured person should never be left alone in the backcountry unless there is absolutely no other way of obtaining help.

At the other extreme, a large group is not usually conducive to pleasant backpacking. As the group gets larger, it becomes more difficult to keep everyone together on the trail, to satisfy everyone's per-

Eleven items that should be carried on every hike: light nylon cord, map, compass, first-aid kit, small flashlight, candle (for starting fires), emergency food, matches in a waterproof container, knife, large square of plastic or a Space Blanket, and extra clothing such as a down-filled vest or sweater and wind/rain jacket.

sonal wishes, and to find suitable campsites. The wilderness experience seems to bring out both the best and the worst in people, and, unless the group is chosen carefully, backpacking with a crowd can be a very trying experience.

Whatever the size of the group, it is usually best to try to keep everyone together while hiking. In unfamiliar country it is all too easy to take the wrong fork in the trail, become separated, or have a straggler become injured with no way of notifying other members of the group if the party is split up. For safety's sake, stay together.

To keep the group together, the hiking pace must be suited to all. A pace that is either too fast or too slow will be very tiring and a burden on everyone. A pace should be selected that will allow you to walk at a fairly constant rate for the entire day. The typical problem for children and beginners is to select an early pace that is entirely too fast. This leads to exhaustion long before the day's objective has been reached. A good rule is to select a pace at the beginning of the day that seems just a little too slow. This can be increased as the day progresses if necessary and yet remain within the capabilities of the group.

If the pace is correct, you should be able to hike continuously with about a 5-minute break each hour and an occasional longer rest stop for lunch or picture taking. If the trail becomes steep, more frequent "breathers" will be required, but these should not be considered full-fledged rest stops. Instead, simply pause in the trail every few minutes and breathe deeply until you recover from the effort of climbing. It is helpful during these pauses to look for a convenient tree or rock to lean against so as to lift the weight of the pack from your shoulders, rather than stopping to actually remove the pack.

If it is impossible to maintain a pace that is suitable to all members of the party, you may decide to split the group, but only with the understanding that everyone will stop and wait at each branch or junction in the trail so there is no possibility of anyone taking the wrong turn. These instructions must be understood by all, and arrangements should be made as to what to do if someone does not reach a meeting point within a reasonable length of time. This point is very important.

The problem can best be avoided altogether by selecting hiking companions of roughly equal ability and physical condition.

Walking techniques vary from one individual to another, but two basic principles should be kept in mind. First, always try to walk so the entire surface of the foot (sole and heel) makes contact with the ground. This is especially important when walking uphill, and, if necessary, it is best to "tack" up the hill by walking back and forth at slight angles rather than walking straight up it on your toes. When the heel is unsupported, the strain on the calf muscles increases tremendously and leads to cramping and fatigue. Experienced hikers also look for convenient rocks or other slight bumps to support the heels

Walking uphill on your toes with your heels unsupported can lead to fatigue and cramping in the calf muscles.

Experienced hikers will try to support the heel whenever possible while walking uphill. It may mean picking and choosing your steps carefully, but it does cut down on fatigue and cramping.

when going uphill, but care must be taken to avoid stepping on anything that is not solid and may slip.

A second energy-saving rule is never step on anything you can step over, and never step over anything you can step around. Such a practice will allow you to maintain a more efficient pace and will eliminate many big steps and unnecessary lifting of the pack, which is very fatiguing.

On any backpacking trip, numerous situations will arise in which sound judgment must be exercised when making decisions. In these situations, there is but one rule: If you must make an error in judgment, make it by being too conservative.

Foot Care

Perhaps more backpacking trips have been ruined by foot problems than by any other single cause. This is unfortunate, because the majority of such problems can be eliminated by sound foot care.

Toenails should be trimmed short and straight across to avoid cutting into adjacent toes, and the feet should be kept clean and dry at all times. Wet feet are prone to blister, so if they should become damp it is well worth the trouble to stop and change into dry socks. Many experienced hikers carry three pair of inner socks. One pair is worn, one pair is kept dry in the pack, while the third pair is washed and hung on the packframe to dry. In this way, clean, dry socks are always available.

Feet should be washed often on the trail, but avoid letting them soak

too long, which will soften them and allow blisters to form. It is also a
good idea to carry a small container of medicated foot powder that can
be applied frequently to keep the feet dry and to avoid athlete's foot.

At the first sign of any irritation or "hot spot" on the foot, stop and
inspect the painful area. If a blister has not formed, a patch of moleskin or thin foam plaster should be applied. Lacking these, a large
piece of adhesive tape should do the trick.

If a blister has formed, wash the area thoroughly and apply an antiseptic. Sterilize the point of a pin or needle in a match flame, and
puncture the blister by inserting the needle through the skin at its
edge. Remove the needle and gently press the blister to drain the fluid.
Immediately apply additional antiseptic, and cover the area with a
sterile dressing. Don't attempt to remove the dead skin, but leave it
intact to allow new skin to form underneath. This will eliminate a
great deal of pain and reduce the possibility of infection.

Insects

In many parts of the country, the most vexing problem faced by the
backpacker is not bears, snakes, rain, or cold, but plain old bugs. Many
trips have been ruined for the novice unable to cope with the clouds of
mosquitoes, black flies, no-see-ums, and other insects that are frequently encountered. To the hiker who is prepared, however, such pests
need be no more than a passing nuisance.

The first line of defense against all types of insects is the proper
clothing, including long pants and long-sleeved shirts that can be
tightly closed at both the neck and the cuffs. In extremely buggy areas,
a headnet is also valuable and, of course, a tightly screened tent is an
absolute necessity. And no hiker in bug country should be without an
adequate supply of insect repellent. Many products of various types
are available, and different brands seem to be more effective for some
individuals than others. For me, two of the best have been Cutter's and
Johnson's Deep Woods Off (a different product than the original Off).

Two new products have just been developed that may revolutionize
the solution to the bug problem. One of them, E-Z Oral Mosquito Repellent (Cordova Laboratories, 13177 Foothill Boulevard, Sylmar, California 91342), is a tablet that is taken by mouth. The product causes
the skin to emit an odor that cannot be detected by anything but mosquitoes. It is safe for children, has no side effects, and is said to be
effective for up to 12 hours.

The Shoo-Bug jacket is made of lightweight, but sturdy, netlike material that is saturated with insect repellent. It's cool and comfortable to wear.

The second product, Shoo-Bug, is a netlike hooded jacket that the user treats with the latest in chemical repellents (supplied with the jacket). The jacket fits comfortably over other clothing, is lightweight and cool, and offers effective protection against every type of insect that is usually encountered by the outdoorsman. The jacket is manufactured by Cole Outdoor Products of America, Inc., 801 P. Street, Lincoln, Nebraska 68508.

Snakes

Despite their fearsome reputation, poisonous snakes are rarely a problem for most backpackers. To be sure, such venomous reptiles are dangerous, but the alert hiker has little to fear if a few obvious precautions are observed.

Before beginning a trip in strange country, it is a good idea to question natives of the area about the presence of snakes along your route. When hiking in known snake areas, avoid plunging headlong through thick underbrush, reaching into logs or other crevasses, and stepping over logs or rocks without looking on the other side. Care should be taken around old buildings, loose boards, and piles of firewood that could harbor the reptiles.

In snake country, a snake-bite kit should always be in your pack, and it is wise to carry a hiking staff and wear long, loose trousers. Since most snakes will avoid man whenever possible, many hikers try to make a little extra noise in places where snakes may be located.

In recent years a variety of snake-bite treatments have been proposed, but the most effective remains the old "cut and suck" method recommended by the Red Cross. The bitten body part should be immobilized in a position below the heart, and, if an arm or leg, a snug constricting band placed 2 to 4 inches above the bite, i.e., between the bite and the heart. But the band should not be so tight that the circulation of blood to the extremity is impaired—just snug.

Sterilize a blade in a flame, and make a shallow $\frac{1}{4}$-inch incision over each fang mark parallel to the long axis of the body part. Do not make an "X" type cross cut, and be certain to cut only deep enough to just penetrate the skin so no damage is done to the underlying tissues.

Apply suction to the wounds for 30 to 60 minutes with the suction cups from your bite kit, or your mouth, being careful not to swallow the venom and to rinse your mouth thoroughly. Wash the wound with soap and water and apply a sterile dressing. Do not give the victim alcohol in any form, nor allow him to walk out under his own power, either of which will increase the flow of blood and the spread of the poison.

Anyone who expects to travel in snake country should study a more complete description of the first-aid procedures in the latest Red Cross Advanced First-Aid Manual. The above is only a brief outline of the accepted treatment.

Wild Animals

An inordinate fear of animals in the wilderness is completely unjustified. Wild animals fear man and, unless surprised, cornered, or separated from their young, will avoid you whenever possible. Adherence to a few basic rules will eliminate the majority of "animal problems."

Never separate a mother animal from her babies, and never pick up, play with, or cuddle wild animal babies. They are not "lost" and mama is sure to be close by. Never attempt to approach a wild animal too closely, or tease it, or cut off its only avenue of escape. In bear country, never take food of any kind into your tent, not even a candy bar. Packs should be suspended from a tree out of the reach of prowling bears whenever possible. Uneaten scraps and garbage should be burned or placed in airtight containers, and the camp kept scrupulously clean. Cooking and eating should be done away from the sleeping area. When hiking in bear country, loud talking, singing, and other noise will warn the animals of your approach and they will leave. Some hikers like to tie small "jingle bells" to their boots for the same reason.

If an animal is encountered that is "acting strangely," trying to approach you, or in any way looks abnormal, keep away from it as it may be suffering from rabies or otherwise injured, in which case it is very dangerous.

Getting Lost

The fear of becoming lost looms inordinately in the minds of novice backpackers, though this fear is usually needless. A backpacker who has a map and compass, knows how to use them, and sticks to maintained trails faces little danger of becoming lost (see Chapter 11). As experience is gained, you can venture farther from established trails with confidence.

Before traveling in unfamiliar territory, you should study a map to obtain an idea of the "lay of the land" in terms of general directions, mountain ranges, valleys, watersheds, roads, and trails. You should set mental boundaries to the area in which you'll be hiking, and plot emergency "escape routes" should you become lost. While hiking, continually be on the lookout for landmarks such as mountain peaks, streams, trail crossings, and lakes to confirm your position.

If you suddenly discover that you cannot recognize a prominent landmark, or something appears to be drastically out of position, you should stop and calmly try to orient your map to known features. In most cases, this will be all that is required to determine if you are where you belong. If you find that you are not, try to mentally reconstruct your backtrail to discover where you may have taken the wrong turn. If this solves the problem, a little backtracking will remedy the situation.

On the other hand, if nothing looks familiar, and your compass confirms that everything is "running the wrong way," you still may not be lost, but merely confused. If you are on a well-marked trail, simply turn around and head back the way you came, keeping a lookout for something you recognize from the map. If you're on a good trail, you will either discover where you made your mistake, come to a trail marker or some other landmark that can be located on your map, or meet other hikers who can tell you where you are.

In case you really are lost, your major enemy is panic. The average backpacker, if he carries the essential items listed earlier and keeps his wits about him, has the means to survive in the woods for a considerable length of time, and will most certainly be found. On the other hand, if fear and panic prevail, the end result could be an unnecessary tragedy.

You should read a good book on survival techniques, and should plan ahead for the time when you may need such information. The time will probably never come, but if it does you will be prepared.

When you become completely lost with no prospect of getting out before dark, collect a pile of firewood, make an emergency shelter, and prepare to make yourself as comfortable as possible for the night. You will undoubtedly be missed when you do not return at the planned time, and a search will be started. Therefore, *stay where you are, and let the party find you*! Don't prolong your stay in the woods by moving from place to place. Otherwise the search party will only find where you've been, not where you are.

If you are with a group, don't split up. Stay together and, if possible, prepare some type of emergency signal such as three smoky fires that will attract attention to you. (Remember, three of anything is the universal emergency signal.) Some hikers carry a small whistle that can be blown as a signal. This is probably a good practice as it will carry farther than your voice and will last longer.

Carry emergency equipment, keep your wits about you, stay in one place, and you will be found.

Hot-Weather Problems

Summertime heat poses special problems for the backpacker, since the combination of high environmental temperatures and excess body heat produced by the physical work places severe stress upon the body's cooling mechanisms. In response to this stress, sweat production and blood flow to the skin increase, producing a change in the body's fluid balance and an additional load on the circulatory system.

When the body is unable to cope with these stresses, either of three heat-induced disabilities can result: muscle cramps, heat exhaustion, or heat stroke. It is important for the hiker to understand the causes, symptoms, and treatment for each of these conditions.

Muscle cramps, due to the increased water and salt loss from profuse sweating, can usually be prevented by drinking sufficient water and replacing the lost salt. Salt tablets should generally be avoided, since they can cause stomach irritation, nausea, and "internal dehydration." It is best to simply use more salt in your daily diet for this purpose. If you feel that you must use salt tablets, they should be taken with plenty of water or with meals.

Heat exhaustion, a somewhat more serious condition, occurs as a result of blood rushing to the vessels of the skin for cooling at the expense of blood flow to the brain and other organs. Often occurring following several hours of strenuous work in the heat, heat exhaustion causes a rapid or irregular heartbeat, nausea, profuse sweating, and a feeling of light-headedness. The victim may faint, and his skin will be pale and cool. His body temperature will be near normal.

The victim should lie down in the shade with his feet slightly elevated. Tight clothing should be loosened, and he may be given cool drinks (a half glass every 15 minutes) laced with salt (about a teaspoon per glass). If vomiting occurs, discontinue the liquids. Relief will usually occur within 30 to 60 minutes and, if the pulse rate has slowed to under 90 beats per minute, sweating has stopped, and the victim feels recovered, he can usually continue hiking, though at a reduced pace. High-energy snacks should be eaten, and an increased intake of water and salt continued.

By far the most serious of the three hot-weather problems, *heat stroke*—also called "sun stroke"—represents an immediate medical emergency. Sweating will have stopped, and the skin will be very red, hot, and dry. The pulse will be rapid and strong, and the body temperature may exceed 105° F. The victim may suffer a loss of coordination, confusion, and unconsciousness.

Since the condition is life threatening, action must be immediate. Treatment consists primarily of cooling the victim down by almost any means available. He should, of course, be placed in the shade, and most clothing removed. Ideally, he should be completely immersed in the cool water of a stream or lake or, if this is impossible, he should be covered with soaking wet clothing or swabbed with cool water. Alcohol is even better for this purpose, but is rarely available in the field. Fanning the victim with a towel or shirt will increase evaporative cooling,

and massaging the extremities will help to circulate the cooled blood
to the body core to aid in recovery.

The victim should be observed for some time following the reduc-
tion of his temperature in case it should suddenly rise again, and
arrangements should be made to evacuate him for medical treatment.
He should not be allowed to walk out under his own power.

Fortunately, the debilitating effects of excessive heat can be avoided
by a few simple precautions. The major factor in the prevention of all
three problems is the maintenance of a normal body fluid and salt
balance. Food should be salted more than usual, and water should be
drunk to replace that lost as sweat. Under dehydrating conditions, a
person does not adequately replace this lost water based upon his normal thirst, so he must make a conscious effort to drink water in extra
measure while hiking. Also, under typical western conditions (low
humidity and/or high altitude) , the backpacker loses a great deal more
water than is realized, since the sweat evaporates too quickly to wet the
clothing. Under such conditions, small amounts of water should be
drunk at short intervals rather than downing a large amount of water
at one time.

In hot weather, backpackers should wear wide-brimmed hats to
shade the head, as well as light clothing that is cut loose, permitting
circulation of air. Frequent rests in the shade, with occasional stops to
soak the feet in a stream or to wet down the shirt, are also of considerable help in maintaining a normal body temperature.

Cold-Weather Problems

Cold-weather problems can be divided into those involving potential
tissue damage as a result of frostbite or freezing, and those that cause a
lowering of the body's core temperature as a result of excessive heat
loss. The latter condition, known as *hypothermia*, can occur with environmental temperatures considerably above the freezing point.

Injuries due to freezing can be further divided into those that are
superficial ("frostnip") and those involving deeper body tissues (true
freezing or "frostbite") . The latter are much more serious, and it is
important to distinguish between the two as the treatment is different
for each.

As frostnip begins, the affected area first feels extremely cold, but as
the process continues it may become completely numb. The skin over
the area will first appear very red, and will eventually turn chalky

white with a waxy appearance. When touched, the area will feel rather spongy since the surface will be stiff while the underlying tissues are still soft. If treated at this point, little or no tissue damage will occur.

However, if the early warning signs are ignored and the freezing allowed to continue, the area will become very hard with a solid, woody feeling, indicating that the deeper tissues have become frozen. As the condition changes from simple frostnip to freezing, the affected area may suddenly feel warm and comfortable to the victim—a symptom not to be taken lightly. Should this occur, prompt treatment is necessary to prevent serious injury and a real medical emergency.

At the frostnip or superficial stage, treatment involves the rapid rewarming of the area. In the field, this is usually accomplished by the simple method of placing a warm hand over the frostnipped cheek or nose, or by putting the affected hand next to the skin of your own armpit. In the case of toes, the warm abdomen of an understanding companion serves the purpose admirably. Under no circumstances should the body part be rubbed during rewarming as this may compound any tissue damage that has occurred. The part should *never* be rubbed with snow as suggested in one outmoded treatment.

When the rewarming process is complete and normal color has returned to the injured area, hiking can usually be resumed *if the affected area is well covered and protected from further freezing*. If blisters have formed, they should never be opened, but should be loosely bandaged and protected from injury.

Deep frostbite ("true freezing") is practically impossible to treat under field conditions. If it is not possible to treat the condition properly, it is best left untreated until suitable facilities are available. A frozen foot, for example, can be walked on for many hours without further injury. But once the treatment has begun, there can be no turning back until thawing is complete, and, following that, the victim will be in no condition to move under his own power.

The frozen part must be rapidly rewarmed by immersion in water at a temperature of 105° to 110° F (just above body temperature, or quite warm to the touch of nonfrozen skin). Such rewarming is painful and may require at least 30 minutes. During this time, aspirin (or other pain killer) and warm food and drinks should be given to the victim, but alcohol and tobacco should be avoided. Neither has a place in the treatment or prevention of cold-induced injuries, and can compound the problem by their effect on blood vessels.

Dry heat, as from a campfire for example, should not be used to thaw frozen body parts, since the victim will be unable to tell when the area is too hot, and he may burn himself. And, again, the frozen part should never be rubbed or manipulated in an attempt to increase circulation or speed up the thawing process. Exercise of the thawed body part by the victim himself should also be avoided.

When thawed, the frozen area should be kept warm and treated as though it were an open wound or burn. Use no antiseptic, but gently clean the area (if necessary) with soap and water, and apply a loose sterile dressing. The victim should see a physician as soon as possible.

Injuries from frostnip and freezing can be very serious, but, of themselves, are rarely fatal. On the other hand, excess loss of body heat with an accompanying drop in the body's core temperature—hypothermia— is often fatal unless prompt treatment is received.

Man, a warm-blooded animal, must produce and dissipate heat at rates that allow him to maintain a normal body temperature of approximately 98° to 100° F. When heat is lost faster than it is produced, the body's core temperature falls, and if allowed to drop far enough, death results. Conditions that are conducive to massive heat loss are frequently encountered by the backpacker, and all who participate in the sport should have an understanding of the prevention and treatment of hypothermia.

Fortunately, these dangerous conditions are well defined and easily identified. They include environmental temperatures below the mid-50s, wind, and moisture. If any two of these conditions are present, hypothermia may be a threat; and if all three exist, the danger is a certainty.

Temperatures below the mid-50s are not normally dangerous if the hiker is dressed reasonably well. In the presence of wind, however, the effective environmental temperature is greatly reduced, and body heat may be carried away very rapidly (see wind chill chart).

Water conducts heat approximately twenty-three times better than dry air, and when clothing has become wet through sweat, rain, snow, or immersion its value as insulation is lost and the moisture rapidly conducts heat away from the body. The most important factor in the prevention of hypothermia is keeping dry. In cool, windy weather, the hiker must avoid becoming wet at all costs. Since clothing soaked by perspiration is just as dangerous as that which has become wet by other means, clothing should be adjusted while hiking to prevent excessive sweating. Under wet, windy conditions the body loses heat faster than it is produced and the body temperature falls. The problem is compounded if the victim is fatigued and has eaten little food to assist with heat production.

Dressing according to the layer theory provides flexible insulation and warmth. This hiker is wearing fishnet underwear, cotton shirt, heavier wool shirt, and a down-filled vest. His hooded jacket provides protection against wind and rain while the hat prevents heat loss through the head. Various layers can be removed or added depending on the conditions.

As the body temperature falls, various defense mechanisms attempt to conserve heat, but if the loss continues, the body begins massive and violent shivering. At this point the hypothermia victim will begin to lose his coordination; he may stumble, his speech may become slurred, and he may be mentally confused. Any of these signs indicate that the body temperature is falling to the critical level for survival. If further heat loss occurs, the victim may become unconscious, shivering may stop, and, ultimately, respiratory and/or cardiac arrest may occur.

Once the initial symptoms of hypothermia are seen, further deterioration of the victim's condition can be very rapid. Death has been known to occur in less than one hour. Thus, it is urgent to take immediate measures to replace lost body heat and to prevent further loss. The treatment involves three basic steps: sheltering the victim from the adverse weather conditions, removing wet clothing, and rewarming him as quickly as possible.

Any emergency shelter should be utilized, and if a tent is available it should be erected. The victim's wet clothing should be removed, his body dried, and he should be placed into a *prewarmed* sleeping bag as soon as possible. He should never be placed directly into a cold bag as this will merely compound the problem. Care should be taken to provide adequate insulation between the sleeping bag and the ground. If possible, another warm person should get into the sleeping bag with the victim, as skin-to-skin contact provides an excellent heat source. If conscious, the victim should be given hot food and nonalcoholic drinks.

In fairly moderate cases of hypothermia, the victim should make no attempt at further hiking until he is warm, dry, and well fed. If the condition has been severe enough to cause unconsciousness, he should not be allowed to walk out under his own power, but should be transported in the horizontal position if possible. In all cases, he should be observed closely for a sudden relapse.

Deaths due to "exposure" are tragic, and the real tragedy is that in most cases they could have been prevented had the victim been well equipped and had the knowledge to cope with the situation. In this case, the proper equipment is that which will help the hiker meet the conditions that produce hypothermia. He should have adequate clothing for insulation, windproof and waterproof outerwear, and adequate food to provide energy and heat production. Since a vast quantity of heat can be lost through the unprotected head, it is extremely important that a hood or cap be worn. A wool stocking cap is ideal. These items should be carried on every outing, including a day trip, if there is even a remote possibility of encountering the conditions that produce hypothermia: temperatures in the mid-50s or lower, wind, and moisture.

The Big Four

In addition to the first-aid and safety measures discussed above, every backpacker should be trained in the first-aid techniques needed to treat the "big four" emergencies: control of bleeding, cessation of breathing, heart stoppage, and shock. Detailed consideration of these important topics is outside the scope of this book, and superficial consideration of them would be of little value. The beginning backpacker is urged to seek further first-aid training either through Red Cross or other classes or by additional reading.

An excellent book that belongs in every outdoorsman's library, and which can help to meet this need, is *The Outdoorsman's Medical*

Guide ($3.95) by Alan E. Nourse, M.D. (New York: Harper & Row, 1974) .

First-Aid Kit

A backpacker's first-aid kit is a highly personal item that should be tailored to each individual's specific needs. The contents of the kit are dictated by many things, including the length and type of trip, the nature of the country, the number in the party, and special medical needs of the individual.

In most cases, prepackaged "drug store first-aid kits" are of little value to the serious backpacker. Instead, the hiker should design his own kit (s) , taking care to include items suitable to the needs dictated by the above considerations. For major trips, it is a good idea to consult your physician, and ask him for his assistance in prescribing special medications for such things as pain, upset stomach, diarrhea, infections, and colds. Each of these medications should be clearly labeled, and should include specific instructions for their uses. They should, of course, be used only as directed and for their intended purposes.

Where appropriate, the kit should contain, in addition to the usual bandages and antiseptics, such things as an elastic bandage, water-purifying tablets, sunburn cream, insect repellent and "itch ointment," moleskin or foam adhesive for blisters, adhesive tape, snake-bite kit, foot powder, aspirin, and a few safety pins.

Backpacking is a wonderful outdoor pursuit that can be enjoyed by those of all ages. By its very nature, though, it places you in an environment where accidents and emergencies can occur. But such potential dangers should not discourage you from becoming a member of the backpacking fraternity. Rather, they should cause the novice to give thought and planning to his undertaking so he might start down the trail mentally and physically prepared to either avoid the emergencies or to meet them when they are unavoidable.

WIND CHILL

Estimated Wind Speed (mph)	Air Temperature (°F)									
	50	40	30	20	10	0	—10	—20	—30	—40
	Equivalent Temperature (°F)									
CALM	50	40	30	20	10	0	—10	—20	—30	—40
5	48	37	27	16	6	—5	—15	—26	—36	—47
10	40	28	16	4	—9	—21	—33	—46	—58	—70
15	36	22	9	—5	—18	—36	—45	—58	—72	—85
20	32	18	4	—10	—25	—39	—53	—67	—82	—96
25	30	16	0	—15	—29	—44	—59	—74	—88	—104
30	28	13	—2	—18	—33	—48	—63	—79	—94	—109
35	27	11	—4	—20	—35	—49	—67	—83	—98	—113
40	26	10	—6	—21	—37	—53	—69	—85	—100	—116

Wind speeds greater than 40 mph have little additional effect

Little danger for properly clothed person

Increasing danger — DANGER OF FREEZING EXPOSED FLESH

Great danger

This wind-chill chart illustrates the influence of the wind upon heat loss from the body. The values in the table are the effective temperature at a given air temperature (top row) and wind speed (left column).

Notes on Contributors

Louis V. Bignami

Louis Bignami is a native Californian who grew up in the Sierras where he worked as a packer and managed to backpack several thousand miles before graduation from college. He has worked as a field archeologist, teacher, lawyer, and touring tennis player, and is currently a freelance writer. A regular contributor to *Camping Journal*, *Coast Magazine*, and others, he specializes in fishing, backpacking, canoeing, skiing, and outdoor cooking. He and his wife Annette make their home in Martinez, California.

Sam and Linda Curtis

Sam and Linda Curtis live near Bozeman, Montana, and have had extensive backpacking experience in the Rocky Mountain west and New England. Sam is a licensed Montana guide as well as an outdoor writer and photographer. He is a Contributing Editor of *Backpacking Journal* and Camping Editor of *All Outdoors* and has written articles for most of the major outdoor magazines. He has recently authored a book with Norman Strung and Earl Perry entitled *Whitewater!* (published by Macmillan). Linda is an opera singer who's also an avid cross-country skier. The Curtises have conducted mountain, desert, and cold-weather backpacking trips that focus on outdoor skills and appreciation of the environment.

Dave Engerbretson

Dr. Dave Engerbretson lives in Moscow, Idaho, and is an Associate Professor of Physical Education at Washington State University, teaching Human Anatomy and Biological Aspects of Sport. A contributing editor to *Backpacking Journal*, he has extensive backpacking experience throughout the country. He has been a backpacking, canoeing, and fly-fishing guide as well as both a downhill and cross-country ski instructor. A member of the Appalachian Mountain 4,000 Footer Club, his articles have appeared in many national publications.

Don Geary

Don Geary is a freelance writer who lives in New York's Catskill

Mountains. He is an avid hiker as well as a devoted fly-fisherman and spends a great deal of his time in pursuit of trails and trout. No stranger to the outdoors, he has hiked and fished throughout the United States and Canada and has eaten more than his share of freeze-dried foods. He readily admits that he's had few fishless days during his travels.

Martin Hanft

Born in New York City, Martin Hanft was first introduced to backpacking in the Adirondack Mountains a decade ago. Since that time he has hiked the Long Trail in Vermont, the Appalachian Trail, and has spent his recent free time exploring the mountains of New England. A former editor at *Outdoor Life* and *Camping Journal*, he's now living in Rhode Island. He spent the past year searching for the fabled "Rhode Island Rockies" mountain range, reputed by him to be among the highest in North America. He hasn't found it yet.

Jorma Hyypia

Jorma Hyypia, a research scientist turned freelance writer, learned much of his outdoor basics in the forests of New England. During college years his activities included spelunking, skiing, and mountain-style backpacking. Later he crisscrossed the contiguous United States many times with his bride, five cameras, and several tape recorders—documenting wilderness America with more than ten thousand color slides, black and white photos, and 16mm movies. He now goes canoeing and backpacking with his college-bound son, who also aspires to writing.

Clifford L. Jacobson

Cliff Jacobson received his B.S. degree in forestry from Purdue University in 1962 and immediately went to work for the Bureau of Land Management in Coos Bay, Oregon. Now an environmental science teacher in Hastings, Minnesota, he is 36 years old, married, and the father of two. A professional canoe guide, he has canoed many of the rivers of the Midwest and as far north as James Bay, Canada. His interests include backpacking, orienteering, and competitive rifle shooting.

Addenda

Equipment Manufacturers and Distributors

The following companies specialize in backpacking equipment and most have information available on goods and services. In some cases there is a charge for the catalog available (usually deducted from any equipment order you might place with them).

Adventure 16
656 Front Street
El Cajon, California 92020

Air Lift
2217 Roosevelt Avenue
Berkeley, California 94703

Alpenlite
P.O. Box 851
Claremont, California 91711

Alpine Designs
6185 E. Arapahoe
Boulder, Colorado 80303

Alpine Products
1309 Windward Circle
West Sacramento, California 95691

Altra Kits
5441 Western Avenue
Boulder, Colorado 80301

Antelope Camping Equipment
21740 Granada Avenue
Cupertino, California 95014

Eddie Bauer
Third and Virginia
Seattle, Washington 98124

Bausch & Lomb, Inc.
Sporting Goods Division
2828 East Foothill Boulevard
Pasadena, California 91107

L. L. Bean
Freeport, Maine 04032

Bishop's Ultimate Equipment
2938 Chain Bridge Road
Oakton, Virginia 22124

Browning
Route 1
Morgan, Utah 84050

Buck Knives
P.O. Box 1267
El Cajon, California 92022

Camel Manufacturing
329 South Central
Knoxville, Tennessee 37902

Camillus Cutlery
Main Street
Camillus, New York 13031

Camp & Hike Shop
4874 Knight-Arnold Road
Memphis, Tennessee 38118

Camplite Products
2232 Lawrence Street
Denver, Colorado 80205

Camp 7
802 South Sherman
Longmont, Colorado 80501

Camp Trails
P.O. Box 23155
Phoenix, Arizona 85063

Camp-Ways
12915 South Spring Street
Los Angeles, California 90061

Cannondale Corporation
35 Pulaski Street
Stamford, Connecticut 06902

Champion Industries
35 East Poplar Street
Philadelphia, Pennsylvania 19123

Chuck Wagon Foods
Woburn, Massachusetts 01801

Class 5
1480 66th Street
Emeryville, California 94608

Coghlan's Ltd.
235 Garry Street
Winnipeg, Manitoba, Canada

The Coleman Company
250 North St. Francis
Wichita, Kansas 67201

Comfy
Raven Industries
P.O. Box 1007
Sioux Falls, South Dakota 57101

Coming Attractions
6519 76 Street
Cabin John, Maryland 20731

Compass Instrument
104 East 25th Street
New York, New York 10010

Co-op Wilderness Supply
1432 University Avenue
Berkeley, California 94702

Cutter Laboratories
4th and Parker
Berkeley, California 94710

Damart Thermawear
2450 W. Sibley Boulevard
Posen, Illinois 60469

Danner Shoe Mfg.
P.O. Box 22204
Portland, Oregon 97222

Denver Tent
1408 West Colfax Avenue
Denver, Colorado 80204

Donner Mountain Corporation
2110 Fifth Street
Berkeley, California 94710

DriLite Foods, Inc.
11333 Atlantic
Lynwood, California 90262

Dunham Company
Brattleboro, Vermont 05301

Duofold, Inc.
Canal Street
Mohawk, New York 12407

Eastern Mountain Sports
1041 Commonwealth Avenue
Boston, Massachusetts 02215

Edsbyn
234 Westport Avenue
Norwalk, Connecticut 06851

Estwing Mfg.
2648 Eighth Street
Rockford, Illinois 61101

Eureka Tent, Inc.
P.O. Box 966
Binghamton, New York 13902

Fabiano Boots
850 Summer Street
South Boston, Massachusetts 02127

Frostline Kits
Frostline Circle
Denver, Colorado 80214

Gerber Blades
14200 SW 72 Avenue
Portland, Oregon 97223

Gerry
5450 North Valley Highway
Denver, Colorado 80216

Don Gleason's
P.O. Box 86
Northampton, Massachusetts 01060

Gookinaid E.R.G.
5946 Wenrich Drive
San Diego, California 92120

Herter's
RR 1
Waseca, Minnesota 56093

High & Light
139½ East 16 Street
Costa Mesa, California 92627

Himilayan Industries
301 Mulberry Street
Pine Bluff, Arkansas 71601

Hine/Snowbridge
P.O. Box 4059 U
Boulder, Colorado 80302

Holubar
Box 7
Boulder, Colorado 80302

JanSport
Paine Field Industrial Park
Everett, Washington 98204

Kangaroo Products
815 Houser Way North
Renton, Washington 98055

Kelty Mountaineering
1801 Victory Boulevard
Glendale, California 91201

Kelty Pack
P.O. Box 639
Sun Valley, California 91352

Kershaw Cutlery
100 Foothills Road
Lake Oswego, Oregon 97034

Lowe Alpine Systems
1752 North 55 Street
Denver, Colorado 80301

Medalist/Universal
11525 Sorrento Valley Road
San Diego, California 92121

Michael's of Oregon
P.O. Box 13010
Portland, Oregon 97213

Milo Hiking Boots
Dexter Shoe Company
31 St. James Avenue
Boston, Massachusetts 02116

Mountain Adventure Kits
P.O. Box 571
Whittier, California 90608

Mountain Products Corporation
123 South Wenatchee Avenue
Wenatchee, Washington 98801

Mountain Traders
1700 Grove Street
Berkeley, California 94709

Mountain Travel
1398-B Solano Avenue
Albany, California 94706

MT 10
Trak Inc.
Shawsheen Village Station
Andover, Massachusetts 01810

National Packaged Trail Foods
18607 St. Clair
Cleveland, Ohio 44110

Natural Food Backpacking Dinners
P.O. Box 532
Corvallis, Oregon 97330

The North Face
1234 Fifth Street
Berkeley, California 94710

North Woods
P.O. Box 17244
Denver, Colorado 80202

Optimus
652 Commonwealth Avenue
Fullerton, California 92634

Oregon Freeze Dry
P.O. Box 1048
Albany, Oregon 97321

Pacific/Ascente
P.O. Box 2028
Fresno, California 93718

Pacific Specialty
7011 Sunset Boulevard
Los Angeles, California 90028

Perma-Pak
40 East 2340 South
Salt Lake City, Utah 84115

Pinnacle Products
1408 West Colfax Avenue
Denver, Colorado 80204

Plant Deck, Inc.
2134 S.W. Wembley Park Road
Lake Oswego, Oregon 97034

Quabaug Rubber Company
P.O. Box 155
North Brookfield, Massachusetts 01535

Raichle Molitor USA
200 Saw Mill River Road
Hawthorne, New York 10532

Recreational Equipment, Inc.
1525 Eleventh Avenue
Seattle, Washington 98122

RefrigiWear
71 Inip Drive
Inwood, New York 11696

Rich-Moor Corporation
P.O. Box 2728
Van Nuys, California 91404

Rivendell Mountain Works
P.O. Box 198
Victor, Idaho 83455

Rocky Mountain Backpack Tours
P.O. Box 2781
Evergreen, Colorado 80439

Rugged Wear Ltd.
P.O. Box 84
Slocum, Rhode Island 02879

M. E. Shaw & Sons
P.O. Box 31428
Los Angeles, California 90031

Sierra Designs
247 Fourth Street
Oakland, California 94607

Silva Company
P.O. Box 547
LaPorte, Indiana 46350

Ski Hut
1615 University Avenue
Berkeley, California 94703

Snow Lion
P.O. Box 9056
Berkeley, California 94701

Stag Brand
Hirsch-Weis
5203 S.E. Johnson Creek Boulevard
Portland, Oregon 97206

Stebco Industries, Inc.
1020 West 40th Street
Chicago, Illinois 60609

Peter Storm Ltd.
Smith Street
Norwich, Connecticut 06360

Stow-A-Way Sports Industries
166 Cushing Highway
Cohasset, Massachusetts 02025

Summit Tours
P.O. Box 746
Hamilton, Montana 59840

Sun Down Kits
2700 Highland Drive
Burnsville, Minnesota 55337

Synergy Works
255 Fourth Street
Oakland, California 94607

The Tent Works
Camden, Maine 04843

Thermos/King Seeley
Norwich, Connecticut 06360

Norm Thompson Outfitters
1805 Northwest Thurman
Portland, Oregon 97209

Trail Tech
108-02 Otis Avenue
Corona, New York 11368

Trails West Division
Raven Industries
P.O. Box 1007
Sioux Falls, South Dakota 57101

Trailwise
2407 Fourth Street
Berkeley, California 94710

Wilderness Experience
9421 Winnetka Avenue
Chatsworth, California 91311

Vantage Products
P.O. Box 2868
Fullerton, California 92633

Wilson & Company
4545 North Lincoln Boulevard
Oklahoma City, Oklahoma 73105

Vasque Boots
Red Wing Shoe Company
Red Wing, Minnesota 55066

Wolverine Division
Wolverine World Wide
Rockford, Michigan 49351

Wenzel
1280 Research Boulevard
St. Louis, Missouri 63132

Woolrich, Inc.
Mill Street
Woolrich, Pennsylvania 17779

Wigwam Mills, Inc.
Sheboygan, Wisconsin 53081

Organizations That Can Help

The following organizations have information on hand that could prove helpful to you if you're planning to do some backpacking. Just write to them and ask.

Appalachian Mountain Club
5 Joy Street
Boston, Massachusetts 02108

Bureau of Outdoor Recreation
Department of the Interior
18th & C Streets N.W.
Washington, D.C. 20240

Appalachian Trail Conference
1718 N Street N.W.
Washington, D.C. 20036

Environmental Protection Agency
Information Office
Washington, D.C. 20460

International Backpackers Association
P.O. Box 85
Lincoln Center, Maine 04458

Army Corps of Engineers
Public Affairs Office
Chief of Engineers
Department of the Army
Washington, D.C. 20314

National Hiking & Ski Touring Association
P.O. Box 7421
Colorado Springs, Colorado 80907

National Park Service
Room 1013
Department of the Interior
Washington, D.C. 20240

National Wildlife Federation
1412 Sixteenth Street N.W.
Washington, D.C. 20036

Sierra Club
530 Bush Street
San Francisco, California 94108

U.S. Forest Service
Department of Agriculture
Washington, D.C. 20250

Wilderness Society
729 Fifteenth Street N.W.
Washington, D.C. 20005

Publications

There are a number of magazines on the market that feature backpacking. Most carry a continuing stream of how-to features and equipment rundowns, as well as first-person accounts of particular trips and areas. One, *Off Belay*, is designed for mountain climbers and walkers. You should be able to pick them up either at large newsstands or in the specialty shops that cater to backpacking and camping. If you can't find a particular magazine locally, you can write for a subscription.

Appalachia Journal (Semi-annual)
Appalachian Mountain Club
5 Joy Street
Boston, Massachusetts 02108 $5 per year

Backpacker (Bi-monthly)
65 Adams Street
Bedford Hills, New York 10507 $12 per year

Backpacking Journal (Quarterly)
Davis Publications
229 Park Avenue South
New York, New York 10003 $5.95 per year

Camping Journal (Eight times per year)
Davis Publications
229 Park Avenue South
New York, New York 10003 $6.95 per year

Off Belay (Bi-monthly)
15630 S.E. 124th Street
Renton, Washington 98055 $7.50 per year

Sierra Club Bulletin (Ten times per year)
530 Bush Street
San Francisco, California 94108 $8 per year

Wilderness Camping (Bi-monthly)
Fitzgerald Communications, Inc.
1597 Union Street
Schenectady, New York 12309 $6.50 per year

Index